Portrait of a Young Scotsman
a life of Edward Baird

PORTRAIT OF A YOUNG SCOTSMAN

a life of Edward Baird
1904-1949

Jonathan Blackwood

THE FLEMING-WYFOLD ART FOUNDATION
London

Published by the Trustees of
The Fleming-Wyfold Art Foundation
for the exhibition held at
The Fleming Collection, 13 Berkeley Street, London W1
13 April to 12 June 2004

Text © Jonathan Blackwood
ISBN 0-9545137-2-X

Designed and typeset in Minion by Bill Smith
Printed by Inglis Allen, Kirkcaldy

CONTENTS

59 Still-life with Flowers in a Glasgow Jug

PREFACE

Edward Baird is a singular figure in twentieth-century Scottish art. When the dominant trend among his contemporaries was to paint landscapes and still-lifes with bold brushwork and fiery colours, Baird's paintings, many of which are portraits, are minutely detailed and are often almost monochromatic. And while most professional Scottish artists lived in and around Edinburgh and Glasgow or moved south to London, Baird preferred to stay in his home town of Montrose, about seventy miles north of Edinburgh. He sold few works and seems to have relied financially on his mother, with whom he lived for most of his short life. Dreadful health and an obsession with detail meant that he finished no more than forty oil paintings; only a handful of drawings survive. He was a fairly obscure figure when he died in 1949 at the age of forty-five. In the intervening years he has assumed an almost mythical status, not just because he was a great artist, but also because we know very little about him.

Judging from the few who remember him, he was equally shy, cantankerous and obstinate. He had few close friends - the artist James McIntosh Patrick was one - and by all accounts he neither craved nor sought company. He kept pretty much to himself, painting away with microscopically-fine brushes in his little studio in Montrose, or lying on his sickbed with the chronic asthma that blighted his life and career. He is the opposite of the Romantic image of the artist - the ebullient, fancy-dressing figure who is sure of what he is doing and lets everyone know it. Baird even failed to score as the sickly aesthete, for to do that properly one has to live in a big city, where one's absences can be noted. The advantage of being on the periphery of things, though, was that he could develop his singular vision with complete independence.

When a couple of years ago Jon Blackwood mentioned his desire to write a book on Baird, I advised him that that could be a thankless task, since Baird had left almost no trace of himself besides the paintings. Happily, Blackwood ignored me and soldiered on, unearthing all kinds of fascinating information on this curious and brilliant artist. Baird would probably have been horrified to find his life held up to such close examination, but he would surely have admired Blackwood's obsessive attention to detail.

PATRICK ELLIOTT
Senior Curator, Scottish National Gallery of Modern Art

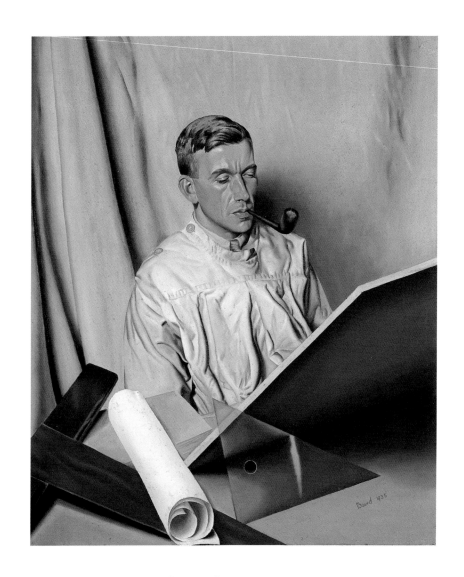

48 GEORGE FAIRWEATHER FRIBA

INTRODUCTION

I first encountered the work of Edward Baird on a visit to Kelvingrove Museum and Art Gallery in Glasgow as an undergraduate in the early 1990s. I was truly captivated by his 1942 painting, *Unidentified Aircraft*. The lighting of the picture, with an unseen bomber's moon and searchlight reflecting off the snow capped Angus hills, is an otherworldly blue-white, which illuminates the striking architectural forms of Montrose and at the same time underlines its wartime vulnerability to attack. This atmosphere of eerie calm and the anxiety of its residents on hearing the sound of an unidentified warplane are subtly understated. The tripartite portrait pushed up against the picture plane, head moving rapidly, hands raised to shield the eyes from the light of the moon and pick out the potential intruder in the sky, is silent testament to the human impact that such raids had.

Intriguingly the gallery was not able to help too much when I asked for further information about the painting. No postcard or slide was available, as no one quite knew who the copyright holder was. Interpretative material was minimal, relying on the account of a Glasgow resident who remembered the painting being completed. A gallery attendant told me:

> No-one knows too much about him. I know he came from Montrose, and didn't often leave there, as his health was very poor. He died quite young and didn't finish many paintings. 'Unidentified Aircraft' is the only painting we have of his – I think there are some others in Edinburgh and Aberdeen. That's about it.

It seemed remarkable that the artist behind this striking painting had left so few traces. Here was a man who had died barely more than 50 years ago, yet who seemed to have left virtually no historical footprint behind. Baird has been thought of as a 'Scottish Vermeer'. As with the seventeenth-century Dutch master, trying to tell Baird's story has been an attempt to piece together seemingly unrelated historical fragments and speculation and producing a coherent narrative. Set alongside the well-chronicled lives of the Peploes, Fergussons, Maxwells and Cowies, this frustrating absence and silence on Baird's work set in motion the research leading to this book and exhibition.

Baird's shunning of publicity during his lifetime and the destruction of most of his personal correspondence and effects after his death in 1949 have made this a particularly challenging and complex piece of research. I must thank the Arts & Humanities Research Board for providing a Small Research Grant to fund my studies. I would also like to thank The Fleming-Wyfold Art

Foundation for generously funding the publication of this monograph and for providing the opportunity to mount an exhibition of Baird's work in the centenary year of his birth.

The staff at the National Library of Scotland, Edinburgh, Montrose Museum, Angus Local Studies Centre, Montrose Public Library and Glasgow School of Art were all very helpful in locating archival material during the course of this project. Staff at the Scottish Public Records Office, The Scottish National Gallery of Modern Art, Edinburgh, Aberdeen Art Galleries, the Imperial War Museum, London, the McManus Galleries, Dundee, Kelvingrove Museum and Art Gallery, Glasgow, Paisley Museum and Art Gallery and the Central Chancery of the Orders of Knighthood, London, provided valuable responses to requests for information.

Graham and the late Jane Stephen in Montrose responded enthusiastically to my research and were immeasurably helpful in providing original source material and access to other individuals who remembered Baird and his work. Fred and Mary Conacher and Mr and Mrs Peter Fairweather offered similar encouragement. Mr Denis Rice discussed the life and work of Fionn MacColla and was very kind in lending rare books on the author for the duration of this project. Bill and Francesca Hardcastle provided access to the letters and effects of MacColla. Mrs Rona Pinterich, Mrs Siñe Machir Grant and Mrs Agnes Valentine were able to offer revealing personal memories of the artist. Christina Reid, reporter at the *Montrose Review*, maintained a sympathetic interest in the project. Other collectors and enthusiasts of Baird gave up significant time and help to my work: Mr Niall Angus, Mrs Marion Fotheringham, Mrs Jean Fraser, Mrs Mary Mackie, Dr. James Morrison, Mrs Valerie Oliver, Mr William Ogg, Ms Liz Ogilvie, Mrs Elizabeth Walker and the Whyte family of Maryland, USA.

Dr Patrick Elliott of the Scottish National Gallery of Modern Art was very generous in providing access to his original research for the Baird exhibition in 1992 and maintained a continual interest in the project. Professor Christopher Green of the Courtauld Institute of Art and Dr. Tom Normand of the University of St. Andrews provided important early help and encouragement.

Finally I must thank the family and friends who all supported me at various stages of the project: my mother and father in Glasgow, Dr. Nigel Blackwood and Bob Bartram in London, James MacKenzie, Gemma Seth-Smith and Gus Young in Edinburgh and my wife, Kath, for her love, support and tolerance of my long research absences from home.

JON BLACKWOOD
University of Glamorgan
March 2004

1. APPROACHING EDWARD BAIRD

Born at Montrose in 1904, Edward Baird studied at the local school, Montrose Academy. It seems that even as a child he suffered badly from the asthma that was to dog him throughout his life. At school he excelled at art, leaving sometime around 1922-23 bitterly disappointed at his failure to secure the art prize. Sometime in his early childhood Baird's father, a ship's master, was lost at sea and his mother was left to bring up Edward and his younger brother, David (born 1906), on her own. It was perhaps the intervention of his uncle, local schoolmaster Walter Graham, which gave Baird the confidence to secure a place at Glasgow School of Art, where he matriculated in September 1924.

Fortunately the details of Baird's studies in Glasgow are much less sketchy. He proved to be the best student in his year, winning a small travel grant in 1926 and then the prestigious Newbery medal and major travelling scholarship the following year. Yet, as we shall see, his choice of destination was to prove unusual. Rather than make the obvious choice and study in Paris, where post-Cubist neo-classicism and Surrealism were the dominant trends, Baird chose to spend four months travelling in Italy, where he made a special study of the Italian primitive painters of the Trecento and Quattrocento. Their meticulous attention to detail and use of jewel-like saturated colour provided a template of perfection that stayed with Baird for the rest of his life. Following his studies, Baird returned permanently to Montrose in 1929.

The artist's passport, issued in October 1928, survives. An unknown official records his physical appearance. Slight at just 5 foot 7 inches, Baird is described as having brown-auburn hair and grey eyes. He meets the gaze of the camera unflinchingly in his photograph with a self-conscious half smile. Photographs of the artist - even from childhood - show him as a pale and slightly stooped figure. Baird suffered from asthma from childhood and was a very heavy smoker as an adult. Frequent episodes of ill health impeded Baird's progress from the late 1920s onward. Many remaining photographs of the artist show him with a cigarette. Ultimately a combination of asthma, chronic bronchitis and cigarettes was to kill him.

James McIntosh Patrick's memoir of his friend, and the recollections of the older residents of Montrose, reveal a meticulous and precise man with a rigorous and uncompromising intellect. At Glasgow School of Art he was nicknamed 'Herr Baird', in part owing to the precision of his speech. In Montrose he was known as 'the Kapitan' for the same reason and also on account of the small boat he used to sail on the River Esk in his leisure time. Some found Baird difficult to get along with.

His dry sense of humour was sometimes a little too barbed, particularly for small children.[1] He was vigorous and stubborn in debate and contemptuous of those who argued from under-informed or illogical positions. He was fiercely idealistic about his work and found it difficult to hide his disdain for fellow artists who did 'potboiler' work to earn money, such as his contemporary, the sculptor William Lamb (1893-1951). It seems that, although Baird had great respect for Lamb's portrait sculpture, he could not overlook the fact that the sculptor produced etched landscapes in a popular style and received an annual grant from 'the County', something which Baird regarded as tantamount to accepting a charity handout.[2]

Further evidence of his unwillingness to compromise is found in the significant relationship in his life - Ann Jeffrey Fairweather (1904-72). Baird became engaged to Ann sometime in 1931, but they did not marry until 1945, as the artist refused to do so without the means to support his fiancée and a new household. Accordingly Baird spent most of his adulthood living with his mother at 121c High Street, Montrose, only taking a studio space in Bridge Street in the second half of the 1930s. Sternly principled and idealist both in his public and private life, it is easy to see why some contemporaries found Baird a little aloof.

Nonetheless Baird was fiercely loyal to his close friends, who were not artists on the whole. These included the local architect, George Fairweather, Ann's brother, and the novelist, Tom MacDonald (Fionn MacColla); professionals such as Allan Ogilvie, a chartered accountant, Tom Whitson, a local solicitor, and newsagent Andrew Dalgetty; and local itinerant workers and sailors who gathered at Montrose harbour, notably Peter Girvan Machir and the poacher, James 'Pumphy' Davidson. All these men knew Baird as a loyal friend who helped in difficult times with many unsolicited acts of kindness and support. The warmth of the tributes paid to him following his death provides ample evidence of that.

Baird died in early January 1949 with barely two decades' worth of oil paintings, drawings and sketches behind him. Apparently he left instructions that after his death all his personal effects - correspondence, unpublished essays, diaries - were to be burnt. This his distraught widow did on the beach at Montrose. As a result there is no archive of Baird's writings, which are normally the first stop for any research project like this. Only around ten unsent drafts of letters, some newspaper cuttings, little used sketchbooks, a satirical radio play and a cache of schoolboy drawings survived the flames. Baird's posthumous instructions created the vacuum of information that has surrounded his work since.[3]

The major themes and interests of Baird's life and work provide us with useful categories in approaching his work. Five major themes emerge: Montrose, its people and way of life; Baird's conception of art and the role of the artist; the relationship between Baird's ideas and those of a hegemonic modernism; the Scottish Literary Renaissance of the 1920s and 1930s; and his commitment to both socialism and Scottish nationalism.

Baird was highly sceptical of the notion of an artistic 'career' and showed no interest in building a celebrity artistic persona. His return to Montrose in April 1929 saw him re-engage with a local rather than national culture. He rarely gave interviews to the press and when he did it was to local papers such as the *Montrose Review* and the *Angus and Mearns Herald*. Although his work featured in national journals such as *Burlington Magazine* in the 1930s, a personal statement did not accompany such articles. It seems that the notion of moving to the metropolitan centres of Edinburgh or London to become involved in the pre-existing art world infrastructure of galleries, dealers, clients, critics and the avant-garde did not occur to him.

On the face of it his return to his home town was tantamount to suicide for a professional artist. Montrose in the late 1920s was a small town of some fifteen thousand inhabitants, reliant on maritime trades, light industry and seasonal tourism for its survival. The *Montrose Review* acknowledged this in 1925, when it opined that 'The East Coast of Scotland is a bleak clime for budding genius, and the plants that have blossomed there into artistic fame are not over many'.[4]

Yet Baird's return to Montrose was no perverse rejection of the art world for its own sake. His decision to return had many motivating factors, aside from obvious family concerns. The first was a technical one. James McIntosh Patrick tells us that Baird's painterly methods were based on a comprehensive knowledge of his subject. He would spend weeks reading up on a subject before he felt able to paint it properly. Baird would then draw very slowly, with the representation of a hand taking him the same amount of time that McIntosh Patrick took to complete a whole figure.[5]

In the people and the features of Montrose Baird had a set of subjects that he had grown up with to use in his art without the need for further exhaustive research. In all his representations of his home town a self-consciously historical vision is employed. For example, in early works such as *Figure Composition with Montrose Behind* (cat.nos. 31 & 32) dated 1927, Baird uses the motif of the old Montrose suspension bridge, which in fact had been demolished and replaced the previous year. His figure paintings continually exhibit a studied class-consciousness. In this drawing the two ploughmen in the right foreground are set apart from the group of agricultural labourers in the middle ground. Baird's unique fusion of deep historical knowledge, awareness of even subtle social distinctions between the people of Montrose and a desire to represent contemporary reality as everyday people understood it in an idiom of craftsmanlike beauty underpinned his developing vision. The realisation of such a vision would not have been possible in an unfamiliar environment.

It must not be assumed that Baird's relative isolation in Montrose meant that he was isolated from contemporary developments in the visual arts. From his days as a schoolboy at Montrose Academy he had been encouraged to read as widely as possible on painting and no doubt took full advantage of the well stocked library at Glasgow School of Art and its collection of contemporary periodicals. The few remaining items of his personal library suggest that he was at least an infrequent reader of serious art periodicals such as *Burlington Magazine* and *The Studio*. On excursions to London and Edinburgh for the purpose of exhibiting his work at the Royal Scottish or Royal Academies, Baird lost no opportunity to view contemporary exhibitions.

All this allowed the development of an informed scepticism regarding the theory and practice of modernism. In the longest exposition of his views on art still extant, Baird longed for an art that existed to delight the viewer and serve as an integral part of daily life, where:

> Art worked in blissful ignorance of its own nature. It believed it was only a trick in the amusement and service of mankind, and existed to paint flowers to deceive bees, to celebrate feats of arms, to adorn council chambers, to charm away melancholy and to teach and improve the people.[6]

This Ruskinian view of the purpose and function of art is contrasted with contemporary discourses surrounding modernism:

> In the mere twittering which passes for thinking in the art world at the present time no theory is too silly or too devoid of contact with reality, no idea too packed with error or irrelevance, no argument too self-contradictory, too hazy at the moment of speaking, too illiterate, provided it sounds clever or imposing.[7]

The choked heaviness of Baird's denunciations here give us some idea of his impatience with pseudo-scientific formalist narratives of art. It would be a mistake, however, to suppose that Baird was an arch conservative and uncompromising opponent of anything other than academic art. In many paintings, such as *Birth of Venus* (47) of 1934, Baird explicitly borrows from the language of English Surrealism as practised by painters such as Edward Wadsworth and Paul Nash.

Baird was no surrealist, however. It seems that he employed at various points some formal idioms of modern art in order to re-enforce his personal quest for disinterested and unselfconscious beauty. Stylistic borrowings from the European 'Call to Order' of the 1920s and Surrealism re-appear continually in both large-scale work such as *Birth of Venus*, and in small-scale imaginative compositions such as the 1943 piece, *Harlequin* (69). Baird considered that the drift of art from representation towards the self-referential styles of abstraction was a tragedy,

31 FIGURE COMPOSITION WITH MONTROSE BEHIND

as it was a false approach to his idealised conceptions of 'beauty' and 'truth', and made art irrelevant to all but a tiny fraction of the audiences who viewed it. Seen in this light, his decision to work in Montrose is entirely understandable.

There was another compelling reason to return to Montrose at the end of the 1920s. Throughout the decade the town had been a key venue in the development of the Scottish Renaissance. This was predominantly a literary movement, with the poet Hugh MacDiarmid (Christopher Murray Grieve, 1892-1978) prominent in its development. MacDiarmid lived in Montrose from 1919 to 1929, editing the *Montrose Review* as well as ceaselessly proselytising in both poetry and critical essays for his vision of a reawakened Scottish culture. As we shall see in the third chapter, a remarkable group of writers, artists and musicians flocked to MacDiarmid's banner in this period with many settling in Montrose. Novelists of the calibre of Edwin and Willa Muir lived in the town, with the composer Francis George Scott a frequent visitor, most memorably when he helped MacDiarmid to finish *A Drunk Man Looks at the Thistle* at the poet's home at 16 Links Avenue in 1926.

MacDiarmid's ideas found political as well as cultural expression in this period. In 1928 he was a founding member of the National Party of Scotland, serving on the party's first National Executive Committee.[8] Soon a lively local branch of the NPS was formed in Montrose and contested elections with reasonably creditable results between 1929 and 1932. MacDiarmid's call for a re-invigorated, confident, avowedly Scottish culture, casting aside Victorian kailyard stereotypes and re-engaging as an equal cultural partner with continental Europe, was a powerful attraction for Baird. For a brief period Montrose was at the forefront of the developing Scottish nationalist creed and Baird became fully involved alongside friends such as MacColla, Ogilvie, Machir and Dalgetty.

Yet by 1929 the first flowering of the Scottish Renaissance was beginning to wither in Montrose. The collapse of MacDiarmid's marriage to Margaret Skinner saw him depart for London after some years of financial uncertainty exacerbated by his drinking habits. With MacDiarmid gone, the Montrose Burghs branch of the NPS foundered in continual disputes with party headquarters in Edinburgh. All the early energy and excitement surrounding the branch seemed to dissipate after the Montrose Burghs by-election in summer 1932.

By this stage Baird was fully identified in the press as a 'Scottish Renaissance' artist, even although his relationship with the movement was somewhat tangential. There is no record of him ever having met MacDiarmid and no reference by the poet to Baird's art in any of his voluminous critical writings. It seems probable that Baird just missed MacDiarmid's departure in 1929 and they are likely to have met for the first time in the early 1930s. Baird is also absent from well-known narratives of the Scottish Renaissance period by Maurice Lindsay and Willa Muir.[9]

There is no doubt, however, that the themes of the Scottish Renaissance and the developing political discourse of Scottish nationalism were to exert a profound influence on Baird's art. His now lost portrait of Fionn MacColla, *Portrait of a Young Scotsman* (40), was bought by the Scots-American nationalist and cultural entrepreneur, James H. Whyte, from the Royal Scottish Academy show of 1932. By this stage Whyte was attempting to give new life to the renaissance movement from his base in St. Andrews. He helped Baird to find at least one portrait commission in the university town.

Increasingly the economic depression of the 1930s and the mass unemployment that followed impacted heavily on the vision of an artist determined to reflect the times in which he lived. The 1936 canvas, *Distressed Area* (51), is a bleak representation of an idle Montrose harbour with a boarded-up hut at the centre of the painting. In this period many exiles from heavy industry in both Glasgow and Dundee passed through Montrose looking for seasonal work. Frustrated at the inability of the Scottish nationalists to address these concerns in a meaningful way, Baird increasingly involved himself in his local Workers' Education Association, trying in some small way to alleviate the hardship experienced by many during that period. Thus began his involvement in community organisations in Montrose and a commitment to a decentralist conception of socialism which endured for the rest of his life.

In many ways the war years provided Baird with the opportunities to achieve a mature synthesis of all his interests in art. He continued with his WEA work and also served on the Committee for the Encouragement of Music and the Arts, helping to organise two major wartime exhibitions of contemporary art in Montrose. A 1942 exhibition with five other Scottish painters at Reid & Lefevre's gallery in London led to his appointment as an official war artist and a series of portrait commissions of Scottish munitions workers. Baird's status as a war artist enabled him to apply for a sketching pass and he completed many pencil studies of Spitfire fighter aircraft at RAF Montrose. By his own slow standards Baird was at his most prolific during 1939-44, producing fourteen oil paintings, two watercolours and seven pastel or chalk portrait studies - nearly a third of his career output. Wartime socialism, providing a clear documentary purpose for the artist, and his active part in the cultural defence of Scotland against a foreign aggressor seems to have suited him.

Sadly, Baird's health cut short this fertile period of creativity. He spent most of the second half of 1944 in hospitals in Montrose and Aberdeen with severe pneumonia and bronchitis.

He married Ann in January 1945, the ceremony conducted at 121c High Street. He then immediately took off his suit and returned to bed. The marriage had finally taken place, as there were real fears at this point that the artist would not recover from his illness. Baird's mother allocated the newly-weds four rooms in her home, but kept a close watch on his health.

In the four years that remained to him, Baird was continually searching for ideas which would allow him to complete a large-scale figurative composition before his death. In fact he was to complete only one more canvas, the landscape *Angus and Mearns* (82), which took a year to complete and was handed over to its purchaser in 1948. Monumental conceptions such as *Museum Piece* (81) and *The Howff* (78) were worked on intermittently between 1945 to 1948; at his death these remained either unfinished sketches or partially-completed fragments.

Baird was quickly forgotten after a successful and well-received memorial exhibition at the Victoria Galleries in Dundee in 1950. Ann managed to sell some of his work after this exhibition. The remainder stayed in her small Montrose flat until her death in 1972. Subsequently the paintings have remained in a small number of private collections in Angus and Perthshire, appearing fleetingly in two local exhibitions in 1968 and 1981 and in a major retrospective organised by Patrick Elliott at the Scottish National Gallery of Modern Art in 1992.

This brief biographical account of Baird asks as many questions as it answers. It reveals a man with a decidedly classicist vision, yet sharpening his vision with a contemporary and politically-engaged cutting edge. It reveals a man determined to make an impact on internationalist discourses of visual culture from an undeniably provincial base. His small body of work provides moving evidence of a lifelong ambition to realise truth and beauty in two dimensions, a struggle conditioned by an insistence on thorough research, a slow perfectionism of technique and cruelly imperfect health. In the centenary year of the artist's birth, the critical reflection that follows is not merely commemorative, but a necessary reconnection of Baird's vision with broader discourses of twentieth-century Scottish art and culture.

2. BEGINNINGS, TRAINING AND TRAVEL
1904-1929

Edward MacEwan Baird was born on 14th December 1904 at 45 High Street, Montrose. He was the eldest son, named after his father, Edward MacEwan Baird. His father and mother, Agnes Brechan, had married in Montrose in 1901. Baird senior was the last of six generations of seafaring Bairds from Montrose; he was a ship's master and apparently was away from home for long periods. Agnes had grown up in nearby Laurencekirk. A second son, David, was born in 1906. Sometime after that Captain Baird was lost with his ship off the coast of Brisbane.[1] Sadly attempts to find out more details of Baird's father - from local newspaper archives and National Maritime Records - have failed to shed any further light on the circumstances or date of his death.

Baird's father had probably died by about 1909, the date of the first photograph of the artist. This is an informal Edwardian portrait, possibly taken behind 45 High Street. Aged five and already in his characteristic stooped pose, the future artist sits at his mother's knee. His physical likeness to his mother, resplendent in her Sunday best, is apparent, as is his rather unhealthy pallor. His younger brother David was much darker and seemed to take after his father.

Agnes Baird left 45 High Street behind after the loss of her husband and set up house at 121c High Street, next to Montrose Town Hall and diagonally opposite the dominating spire of Montrose Old Kirk. The flat was above the new Montrose telephone exchange, recessed into the corner of the town's remarkably broad main thoroughfare. It was here that Edward Baird was to live for most of his life. The main windows of the flat give a commanding view of the High Street and many older Montrosians remember seeing Baird perched by the window sill as an adult, observing the comings and goings from the shops and businesses below.

The new Baird home was a two minutes walk from Montrose Academy, where he would have started school around the time of the 1909 photograph and continued until at least 1922. Precise dates are impossible to establish. It was during this period that Baird's interest in art began to develop seriously. Contemporary school magazines reveal a spacious, well lit and well stocked art room.[2] Under the sympathetic guidance of a young art teacher, Miss Lena Gaudie (later Mrs Lena Cox),[3] Baird learned the basics of freehand drawing, watercolour and pastel. During the course of the author's research a small cache of Baird's schoolboy drawings, dating from 1915-17, was discovered. They give a fascinating insight into his early development.

SCHOOL DRAWINGS c.1917

Baird seems to have focused on still-life in his art class. The drawings reveal a mixture of objects from the art room, branches and flowers. In a 1915 drawing of a pot, Baird, then aged eleven, rather hesitantly tries to work out the fall of light on the object with a series of anxious shading hatches. The outline of the pot has been worked over several times, as though he lacked confidence in his original drawing. It seems that his streak of perfectionism was with him from an early age. Over time his confidence in pencil drawing increased significantly. A later drawing of an oil carrier captures the difficult lines of the object with grace and sensitivity, displaying none of the earlier self-doubt.

Only one figurative drawing survives from this period - a pencil study of an equestrian statue. This is a rather odd anatomical piece. Baird seems to have focused on the horse for most of the drawing with the figure seemingly added on as an afterthought. Baird shows more interest in experimenting with the appearance of the figure's torso and is less concerned about how it relates to the animal. Comically he runs out of space at the top of the page and includes a careful pencil study of the figure's head alongside the main drawing. As there was no equestrian statuary for Baird to respond to in Montrose, the drawing shows us that he was encouraged to study closely the magazines and art books in the Montrose Academy library and to make studies after reproductions of interest. Baird's Chinese-style drawings of tree branches, dating from 1917, provide further evidence of a wide-ranging and curious intellect.

The most interesting of these early drawings, however, is a heavily-shaded portrayal of a sea shell. It reveals the boy's increasing mastery of light, shade and line. The fading of light into darkness at the shell's opening is beautifully rendered; the irregular grooves and markings and patterns of light and shadow are painstakingly observed. This drawing shows us that Baird was very experienced in the technique of working slowly with an ultra sharp HB pencil well before his matriculation at Glasgow School of Art.

Baird's mature output was based on thorough research and a profound understanding of his subjects. In this sense his school experience is important as it provided him with a series of motifs and subjects on which he would draw during his later career. Exactly the same sea shell re-appears in the 1934 painting, *Birth of Venus* (47), next to the portrait bust in the right middle ground. It is tempting to speculate, too, that the portrait bust in this painting dates from Baird's school days. This stage of his development is significant as it marks the foundation of Baird's visual memory and a growing intellectual development in his understanding of the objects he represented. In the relationship between the sea shell drawing and *Birth of Venus* we finally have evidence of the critical link between visual memory and representation in his art.

During 1917 Baird began to experiment consistently with both watercolour and pastel. This passage of enquiry began with some intense washes being applied to drawings of branches and leaves. In a drawing of a hawthorn branch Baird seems to respond to the techniques of Chinese water-colourists in his angular stylisation of the branch and the contrast of the deep brown branch with little pigments of berry-red. This 'Chinese' influence extends to other similar drawings of still-life items, in particular the art-room bellows and his rendition of what appears to be a Chinese or Japanese fan. In this latter study we can see a further development. The outline of the fan is similar to the pencil drawings discussed above, but here the line is more assured. The pattern of the flower decoration is deftly handled with each leaf and petal meticulously described. This drawing would also have given Baird confidence in the handling of colour. The intense red used here in a confined pictorial space has a powerful effect.

From the art historian's point of view the thread of Baird's development snaps frustratingly here and the years between the end of 1917 and 1923 are missing. But of course focusing merely on his development as an artist would neglect other important aspects of his life. At Montrose Academy Baird met many of the people who were to be close friends in later life and subjects in his paintings. His future wife, Ann Fairweather, had been born six weeks before him on 31st

October 1904[4] and they would have met in childhood at school. Just as important was Ann's younger brother, George, born in 1906, who was to go on to become a successful architect and whom Baird painted in 1935.[5] Baird also met Dan Crosse, another future subject, and Thomas MacDonald, who as Fionn MacColla wrote the Scottish Renaissance novels *The Albannach* and *And the Cock Crew*. During his childhood and adolescence Baird was also to benefit from support and advice from his Uncle Walter Graham, headmaster of the now long-closed Craig School in the hills behind Ferryden.[6]

Graham undoubtedly filled the huge gap left in the boy's life by the death of his father. As Graham was married to Baird's aunt, it is very likely that he would have seen his uncle very often. Many of Baird's paintings of Montrose - such as *Figure Composition with Montrose Behind, Monros* (55), and *Unidentified Aircraft* (68) - were imagined from a vantage point on a hill overlooking Montrose and Ferryden near Craig School. This suggests that Baird spent time sketching in the area around his uncle's home, perhaps actively encouraged to do so.

When Baird left school there was no question of him following his father to sea on account of his asthma. This is likely to have disappointed the artist, as he was keenly aware of his family history and, as McIntosh Patrick points out, had a lifelong interest in boats and sailing. We have no remaining evidence of the thought processes that led to his attendance at Glasgow School of Art. All that remains is a tantalising fragment in a little-used sketchbook of the direction of his life in the early 1920s. Written in the third person, this half page dramatised account of a young man seeking employment in Montrose - 'a sober youth, reserved for his years' - may well be based on personal experience. Baird mentions work with a rope and sail maker at Montrose harbour and he may have sought to make a living there between 1922 and 1924. However the ropemaker is long gone and thus there is no way of telling whether this is based on fact or entirely made up.

We do know anecdotally that Baird did not win the art prize in his final year at school and this was a cruel disappointment to him. He may well have taken work for a time to consider his future. Walter Graham and his mother would undoubtedly have encouraged him to apply for art school, but problems regarding the payment of fees would have been to the forefront of such discussions. As a widow, Baird's mother was unlikely to have been able to fund his studies on her own and there is no record of Baird having received any scholarship. During his studies fees were set at £16 per annum with further sums required to cover accommodation, material and equipment. It seems fair to assume that his family encouraged the disappointed Baird to apply for art school and jointly scraped together the necessary money.

The earliest surviving Baird oil painting, *Blue Cornflowers in a Dryleys Jug* (26) (1923), dates to this period of uncertainty. It is possible that this painting may have been amongst Baird's

26 BLUE CORNFLOWERS IN A DRYLEYS JUG

submissions to the art school as evidence of his suitability for the course. This is a remarkable study of colour, light and spatial awareness, showing significant development from his juvenile drawings. Baird had clearly been looking at contemporary Scottish still-lifes, as the white table cloth and grey, neutral background increase the intensity of his restricted palette in the still-life objects. This was a technique favoured by Peploe and Fergusson amongst others. Unlike these Colourist painters, however, this painting shows no awareness of contemporary developments in Continental modernism. The objects are faithfully recorded in terms of appearance and colour. The apples tip forward slightly into the spectator's space, lifted up by the folds of the cloth, their colour gently leading the eye on to the clay-brown of the pot. The cornflowers provide a spectacular counterpoint; their deep blue colour attracts the eye and invites us to consider Baird's painstaking indication of their petals, before fading to intangible background shadow. This microscopically-rendered detail may indicate an interest in the miniaturist work of a young Henry Raeburn, and of seventeenth-century Dutch art. The painting shows us an early grasp of composition and an assured handling of colour, light and shadow. Baird was to return to such still-lifes in the early years of the war.

If *Blue Cornflowers* was submitted to the examiners at Glasgow School of Art, it obviously made a deep impression, as Baird was one of only two students admitted by them straight into the second year of the painting degree, missing out first year subjects including colour and lettering. On matriculation in September 1924 Baird found himself lodging in Glasgow's West End with the other direct second year entrant, James McIntosh Patrick from Dundee.

For session 1924-25 Glasgow School of Art had John D. Revel as Director with Maurice Greiffenhagen[7] and R. Anning Bell as Professors of Drawing and Painting. Both professors were regular exhibitors at the Royal Academy annual show and the equivalent at the Royal Scottish Academy in Edinburgh. Greiffenhagen in particular was well known for his highly-decorative figure paintings. At the end of Baird's first year Greiffenhagen was widely praised for his portrait, *Miss Pearl Hood*, exhibited at the Royal Academy. In the same year he completed a striking panel entitled *Empire*, featuring tigers, elephants and Indians in a variety of traditional outfits.

As McIntosh Patrick remembers, Greiffenhagen exerted a significant influence on Baird's year at Glasgow School of Art. He led his students through a traditional education, focusing on drawing from cast and from life, the study of anatomy and perspective, composition, still-life, watercolour and tempera techniques with a small number of lectures on the history of art also included. Many of Baird's contemporaries were to develop a full-time career as an artist on the back of their degrees, including McIntosh Patrick, Sydney d'Horne Shepherd, who became one of the painters associated with the Scottish Renaissance, Ian Fleming, Cecilia Bell and Elizabeth Dewar.

Sadly nothing survives from this period, but a small oil and tempera panel, *Fawn* (27), dates from Baird's second year at Glasgow. The little painting - no more than six by four inches - bears out McIntosh Patrick's observation that Baird's work became increasingly small in scale during his first two years at college. The painting itself shows the fawn outlined against a dark, indeterminate background; it may have been a study after a Renaissance painter such as Botticelli or Piero di Cosimo. This study would have played a part in Baird's first success at art school, namely the award of a Minor Travelling Bursary at the end of session 1925-26. This was an award of £10 to enable

'Minor Travel Bursars [to] go to London or other centre to study for two weeks'.[8] Baird spent his summer in Montrose planning his first visit to London and travelled on 24th August 1926 'by road as passenger in the sidecar of the motorcycle combination of Mr. Scott, the other recipient of a Minor Travelling Bursary'.[9]

Having looked at gallery schedules for 1926, there seems little in the commercial venues that would have held Baird's attention in September 1926. Both he and Scott are likely to have spent time studying at the National Gallery, the National Gallery at Millbank (now Tate Britain) and the Victoria and Albert Museum. Baird is likely to have been impressed by the Renaissance and Dutch collections at the National Gallery and the newly-installed galleries of modern French painting at Millbank.[10] It also inspired a life-long enjoyment of London in the painter; family members recall him describing 'great nights' in London, although they are unsure of the period to which Baird referred.[11]

Baird's first visit to London seems to have inspired him to work on a larger scale again, for in his final year three large-scale compositions survive - a nude and the preparatory sketch for *Figure Composition with Montrose Behind* together with the completed painting. In these latter two near-identical images Baird produces his first large-scale works referring to his home town. The view of Montrose is taken from the hills near Walter Graham's school, portraying a panoramic view across the River Esk to Montrose itself and the Angus hills behind. Interestingly Baird has chosen to draw in the old Montrose suspension bridge at the far left of both works. In fact this bridge had been demolished and replaced by the present one in 1926. Other commentators have speculated that this is evidence of Baird's interest in displaying a historical view of Montrose. The truth is likelier to be that Baird pencilled in the old bridge as he did not know enough about the new version to be confident in including it in a painting.

In both images the tensions between the two groups of figures are clear. The older agricultural labourers in the foreground walk steadily, almost in step, one acknowledging our gaze uneasily, the other seemingly oblivious. The group of younger figures seems to hesitate as they pass by, stopping their jostling game momentarily. In this keenly observed moment a key theme of Baird's art emerges, namely the conflict between a passing tradition of agricultural work and specialised work in factories. These works are the first clear evidence we have of Baird's desire to create monumental figurative compositions on a large scale.

The conflicts between the rural and the urban, and the fundamental changes that Scottish society experienced with the move of workers from the countryside to the city looking for work, were to exercise Scottish Renaissance authors and artists a great deal in the 1920s and '30s. It is the key animating tension behind Lewis Grassic Gibbon's canonical work, *A Scots Quair*, and similarly features strongly in lesser-known novels of the period such as MacColla's *The Albannach* and James Barke's *The Land of the Leal*. In his subtle elevation of the two agricultural labourers above the younger group, and in his distancing of the two sets of figures, Baird shows an awareness of these debates. It is telling that the farm workers are much fewer in number and obviously much older than the younger group. These figures obscure the familiar pin-sharp depiction of Montrose and the River Esk. It almost seems as though there is a silent war of attrition for the future character of the town going on here.

Baird's tempera study of the same scene, identical save for a few small details, is evidence of his growing confidence as an artist, however tortured the completion of this work may have been.[12] His tutors at Glasgow School of Art recognised this, as the tempera version was illustrated in the School's prospectus for 1927-28 above an etching by James McIntosh Patrick.[13] Assessing the students of Baird's year, Sir George Clausen, acting as external examiner, observed that '...the School has at present two or three students of quite remarkable promise, whose composition would give distinction to any school'.[14]

1927 was the year that Baird finally made good his clear potential. For his final year diploma he was engaged in the last months of the session in completing a large-scale nude figure. In the completed work his mastery of anatomy, colouration and light is clear. The woman, hands behind her clutching some drapery, meets our gaze unflinchingly. The painting is lit from the top left hand corner and plays across her face and torso with the legs slowly receding into shadow. In addition to paying homage to Renaissance precursors and demonstrating a mastery of the academic techniques he had learned, Baird's nude is an affecting study of *caractère*. The woman is unselfconscious in her nudity, but there is a tremendous air of melancholy in her features. For this painting Baird won the prestigious Newbery medal, awarded to the outstanding student of each final year. In a year containing many talented rivals this was no easy achievement. More importantly this award, worth £66, paid for Baird to return to art school for a fourth year, to complete teacher training and postgraduate study and from there to set out on a tour of Italy.

Thus for the first time in his life Baird had a measure of financial independence and, with the completion of his teaching diploma during 1927-28, saw his career options broadened. A surviving painting from this diploma year - the small tempera panel *Adam and Eve* (33) - gives evidence of the excitement he must have felt at this time. The panel gives the Biblical story of Adam and Eve a decidedly contemporary twist. The Garden of Eden is shown as confined behind a wall and a classical arch, perhaps making reference to Masaccio's *Expulsion from the Garden of*

(LEFT) *33* ADAM AND EVE
(RIGHT) *35* ROOFTOPS FROM THE PINCIO, ROME

Eden (1427, Church of S.Maria del Carmine, Florence). But in contrast to Masaccio's painting the figures of Adam and Eve seem almost light hearted, Adam gesturing expansively, Eve by his side with a half smile on her face. There is no vengeful angel physically ejecting the pair as is common in pictures of this scene. There is also a strong emphasis on the decorative: in the gentle curve of the pathway, the astutely observed loin garlands and in the overall colour scheme of turquoise and cream. This work revisits a standard Renaissance subject in an almost Art Deco style. The problems with the tempera method that McIntosh Patrick mentions in his memoir are very evident here; the medium has eroded badly over time, largely obscuring the facial features of Adam and Eve.

Baird received a postgraduate diploma at the end of the academic year and was awarded a Travelling Scholarship of £120. This was a major award, enabling the best student of the year to spend a period of four months travelling abroad, studying, sketching and painting. The terms of the scholarship specified a concentration on three types of drawing: drawings from decorations or

27

decorative paintings, drawings of architectural interest and outdoor sketches. An itinerary had to be agreed in advance and a final report submitted at the end of the sabbatical. Previously very little was known about this episode in Baird's life, but surviving letters at Glasgow School of Art tell us a little more of exactly where he went in Italy and his response to it.

Baird spent the autumn of 1928 finalising his itinerary, which he submitted to the art school in November. He chose to travel to Italy to study the Italian primitive painters of the Quattrocento, whose work had influenced his developing student vision substantially. The letter survives and provides a fascinating justification for the artist's choice of country:

> ...In conclusion I wish to study the primitives of the three great schools. I approach them with a certain general knowledge of events, Political and religious, that led to and allowed the evolution of the renaissance cultures in Italy…I find in the Primitives and their Schools a purer and deeper and more direct inspiration than the later masters with more popular accomplishments. I find in the Primitives a lively growing Art, rooted fast in the spiritual soil of their Italy, and paradoxically rendered evident through the physical forms of a simple Italy where the people tilled and herded and span and builded and held their moats and lived and died.[15]

This passage demonstrates Baird's clear commitment to an art rooted in reality, with the lives of ordinary working people as its central focus. Words such as 'simple', 'direct' and 'spiritual' may indicate an affinity with the 'naïve' art made fashionable in 1920s English modernism by the likes of Christopher Wood, Ben and Winifred Nicholson and Alfred Wallis. Yet there is no sentimental or romanticising impulse here. Whereas the Nicholsons and Wood responded in part to the 'primitive' masterpieces of Wallis at St. Ives[16] in an attempt to overthrow the academic training they had received, Baird took the opposite direction. He fully intended to use the academic training he had received to assess the methods and techniques of the Italian 'primitives' as a basis for the representation of the Italy in which they lived. Baird's focus on political and religious matters, in addition to his knowledge of the painting of this period, makes another connection between art and everyday life.

Glasgow School of Art approved Baird's course of study by letter on 7th December 1928 and he embarked on his journey four days later via London and Dieppe, arriving in Rome on the 18th of the month. He took lodgings in the Quartiere Ludovici and seems to have wasted no time starting work. The pencil sketch *Rooftops from the Pincio, Rome: Italian Scene* (35) is dated to 1928 and was probably the first work Baird undertook after his journey. The work shows Baird coping assuredly in pencil with the unfamiliar architectural topography of Rome. The space in the drawing is tightly constrained, with the buildings supplicating themselves in an uncomfortable jumble before the distant cathedral. The cactus plant at the bottom right of the sketch adds an unusual element and locates it firmly in the 1920s. The table-top still-life giving way to a street scene had been popularised in this decade by the painters of the London Group.

Baird had to write regularly to his tutors at the art school to keep them informed of his progress. He seems to have left Rome for Assisi in February 1928 and used that town as a basis for the exploration of central and north eastern Italy. A letter of April 1929 shows that he visited Spello, Foliglio, Derouta, Perugia and Montefalco whilst based in Assisi. Yet only drawings from Assisi itself survive. *Monastery of St. Francis of Assisi* (38) is an impressive architectural study in pen and ink. He also seems to have experimented with the relationship between architecture and the human form in *Italian Scene with Nude* (37). A further study of Assisi, last seen at his memorial exhibition in 1950, is now lost. It is tempting to speculate what else he might have sketched during his visit. For example, he is likely to have visited Montefalco to sketch the huge shipyards and seaplane factory of CANT given his interest in shipping, but unfortunately this cannot be confirmed. Certainly his last two months in Italy were spent sketching out of doors, as a letter suggests:

> The weather has hitherto made out of doors work almost impossible but now (excepting a lapse two days ago into a snow blizzard) has definitely changed towards spring; so that the remainder of my stay in Italy bids to be very pleasant.[17]

Baird also visited Florence and Venice in April-May 1929, but by then his sabbatical was at an end. His passport records that he left Italy for three days in Switzerland from 23rd to 26th May. The purpose of this visit remains obscure. It may have been for health reasons, but it has also been suggested that he visited a relative there.[18] Whatever the reason, he was back in Britain on 27th May. So ended Baird's only trip abroad, although his experiences were to exert a continuing influence on his work for the rest of his life.

He returned to his family in Montrose and seems to have lapsed into illness for much of that summer, as his report on his sketching tour was not delivered to Glasgow School of Art until October of that year.[19] Frustratingly, this report has since disappeared and there is no record of his tutors' response to the work completed in Italy.

Baird's period at Glasgow School of Art decisively overturned any lingering disappointment and self-doubt at having failed to win the art prize at school. In his four years as a student he had built up a small but strikingly original body of work and developed a conception of an art rooted in contemporary reality that he was to follow for the remainder of his career. He had won every prize available to him as a student. His trip to Italy allowed him to come to terms with an unfamiliar classical architecture and to develop a deeper knowledge of the techniques and subject matter of the early Italian renaissance painters. He certainly could not have asked for a more solid platform on which to build an artistic career, if that was what he wanted to do. Yet, as we shall see, the brief flowering of the Scottish Renaissance and the excitement that the emergence of the new National Party of Scotland generated in Montrose were to command his attention for the next few years.

William Lamb
(1893-1951)
EDWARD BAIRD
bronze
(Angus Council
Cultural Services)

3. BAIRD AND THE SCOTTISH RENAISSANCE

Montrose had been in something of a cultural and political ferment since Baird's departure for Glasgow School of Art in September 1924. During his five years in Glasgow and Italy the Scottish Renaissance had gathered pace. Held together by the ceaseless writing, speech making and proselytising of C.M. Grieve's *alter ego*, Hugh MacDiarmid, the ideas of the Renaissance were widely disseminated in Montrose. Grieve became a kenspeckle figure in Montrose, editing the *Montrose Review* until 1929, serving as a Justice of the Peace and local town councillor. MacDiarmid's ideas gained a wider audience through his syndicated articles written for the regional Scottish media. In time these ideas met with sympathetic responses from authors and painters. Montrose novelist, Willa Muir, and her husband, Edwin, lived in Montrose for a period in the 1920s and kept in close contact with the poet. Francis George Scott, sometime English teacher of the schoolboy Grieve in Langholm, kept in close contact and in turn MacDiarmid held up Scott's compositions as examples of a Scottish musical renaissance.

Although the Scottish Renaissance was largely a literary movement, visual culture in Montrose was not left behind, with regular local exhibitions organised by the amateur artist, George Cathro. A painter and decorator, Cathro organised near-annual exhibitions from his premises in Bridge Street, to which William Lamb, Renée Simm and Miss E.D. Mackie were regular contributors. It took some time for ordinary Montrosians to take note of the new cultural forces bursting into life in their town. Reviewing an exhibition of Cathro's work, a journalist noted:

> Few towns of the size of Montrose could bring together such an exhibition and the elements of artistic merit and local and personal interest are so deftly intermingled in this case that Mr Cathro's enterprise well deserves the reward of a little public interest and appreciation.[1]

At the core of the Scottish Renaissance was a desire to re-engage with high culture in Scottish, rather than British, terms. MacDiarmid despised the sentimental chocolate box caricature of Scotland and the Scots popularised in Victorian times by 'kailyard' novelists such as Sir J.M. Barrie and by popular comedians such as Harry Lauder. For MacDiarmid such portrayals produced an infantile, deformed perspective on Scottish identity. In the kailyard Scots people were typically presented as gossiping, thrawn small-town dwellers, their lives concerned with little more than the daily trifles of family and friends, supplicated to the unquestioned moral authority of the Kirk. Scottishness was reduced to a series of amusing and eccentric personality traits leavened by the caprice of local dialect. Kailyard Scotland was easily subsumed by broader discourses of British nationhood and imperial dominance. The kailyard presence in the visual arts can be seen in the Highland landscapes of Horatio McCulloch, typically representing the grandeur of a depopulated landscape, or in the 'soupy brown' genre paintings of George Paul Chalmers. In response MacDiarmid proposed the etcher and illustrator, William McCance, and the painter, William Johnstone, as exemplars of the Scottish Renaissance in the visual arts.

MacDiarmid's challenge to the 'kailyard' view of Scottish nationhood was explicit and unrelenting. He edited a series of short-run cultural and literary periodicals, including *Northern Numbers* and *Scottish Chapbook*. This last journal self-consciously echoed the bold typography and vivid colouration of the pre-war English avant-garde journal *BLAST*. With its brick red cover, lion rampant and slogan 'Not Traditions-Precedents!' *Scottish Chapbook* was one example of a determination to place Scottish culture on a determinedly independent footing with internationalist ambitions. From 1923 onwards his poetry was written in 'synthetic Scots', a hybrid of various local dialects. Through his use of a defiantly Scottish brogue MacDiarmid hoped to synthesize various Scots vernaculars and through this process to reclaim Scottish writing as a whole from the standardising yoke of Britishness. MacDiarmid wanted Scottish artists to reflect upon contemporary Scottish culture and the 'Machine Age', rather than reproducing a glib and barely-understood series of kailyard stereotypes. Such a viewpoint had clear political implications and in the second half of the 1920s this developed with the coalescing of various nationalist groupings into the newly formed National Party of Scotland (NPS).[2]

If Baird was unaware of MacDiarmid as editor of the *Montrose Review*, he would have become aware of him during his time as a student in Glasgow. In 1928 the Glasgow University Student Nationalist Association nominated R.B. Cunninghame Graham as a candidate in their rectorial election in opposition to the then Tory Prime Minister, Stanley Baldwin. MacDiarmid and student nationalist leader, John MacCormick, were heavily involved in Cunninghame Graham's campaign, which missed success by only 60 votes. Whilst rectorial elections today attract little interest, the near defeat of the Prime Minister by a Scottish nationalist would have been a major news story at the end of the 1920s. There was much press coverage of the campaign and of the foundation of the NPS on 11th February 1928,[3] which saw MacDiarmid elected to the first National Executive Committee of the new party.[4] Baird would have been aware of these developments in Glasgow and MacDiarmid wasted no time publicising the new party in the pages of the *Montrose Review*.

A Montrose branch of the NPS was quickly formed and it seems likely that Baird would have joined this. On his return to the town he would have found many of his close friends involved with the party. Andrew Dalgetty served as Honorary Secretary of the Montrose NPS and his newsagent's shop was always well stocked with Nationalist pamphlets and publications. Allan Ogilvie acted as an electoral agent for the NPS in both local and national elections.[5] Anecdotally, older residents of Montrose remember NPS branch meetings being held at Peter Machir's house in Wharf Street. Machir was one of Baird's oldest friends in the town.[6]

Baird's interest in the ideas of the Scottish Renaissance were further stimulated by the return of Tom MacDonald (Fionn MacColla) to Montrose in mid-1929. From a house at 12 Links Avenue MacColla began to write *The Albannach* and seems to have spent a good deal of time with Baird during that summer. In his autobiographical memoir, *Too Long in this Condition*, MacColla makes reference to 'making nationalist propaganda' with Baird during this period. Until very recently this was tantalising speculation, as no 'nationalist propaganda' of any sort from Montrose survives in the Scottish National Party's archives in Edinburgh. Fortunately a copy of a logo (36) made by Baird survives on a letter sent by MacColla to Peter Machir in 1935. Entitled 'No Union', the image is a stylised thistle divided into bold harlequin-style checks. Although the image bears no signature, the capitalised writing is very similar to that of Baird and the logo has since been confirmed as having been designed by him.[7] In this period party political colours and logos were not centrally controlled, as they are today, and it seems likely that this image was used by the NPS until the mid 1930s, when a standard logo of a red lion superimposed on a saltire was introduced. 'No Union' provides new evidence as to the level of Baird's involvement in the Montrose NPS at this time.

With MacDiarmid's departure to London to work with the music paper, *Vox*, in mid-1929 and MacColla's frequent absences in London, St. Andrews and Glasgow, the work of the local NPS fell increasingly to Baird's circle of friends. Not that this interest in active politics meant that Baird had given up on painting. On the contrary he seems to have spent the years 1930 and '31 reading and working towards the two major portraits that were to establish a reputation for him in 1932. We should not assume, given Baird's slow working method, that the lack of completed paintings dating to 1930-31 indicates inactivity.

It is likely that work on the celebrated and sadly now lost *Portrait of a Young Scotsman* (40) began in early 1931 during one of MacColla's many visits to Montrose. MacColla was rather itinerant at this time, shuttling between Glasgow University, Montrose and St. Andrews, whilst drafting *The Albannach*. MacColla's novel tells the story of Murdo Anderson, a Highland crofter's son committed to the Gaelic language and culture in opposition to the repressive, Anglophone doctrine of Calvinism. The book charts Murdo's personal struggle with these contradictory aspects of Scottishness and concludes with his re-settlement in the Highlands and a determination to keep the Gaelic culture alive in that area through his own example. MacColla finally finished the novel in the last weeks of 1930 in a cottage in St. Andrews, rented for him by the cultural entrepreneur, James H. Whyte. Baird would have visited MacColla there and through him met Whyte. The latter had arrived in St. Andrews from the USA in October 1930 and had determined to transplant the energy and creative fertility of the 1920s Renaissance to the university town. The Scots-American was to be an encouraging friend to Baird in terms of commissions and patronage as the 1930s took shape.

No photographic record of Baird's portrait survives. However it was exhibited to favourable comment at the Royal Academy in London in April 1932 and again at the Royal Scottish Academy in Edinburgh the following year. The *Montrose Review*, praising Baird for 'being honoured' in having the portrait 'hung on the line' at Burlington House, identified the ideas that lay behind the work:

> Here, the artist has accomplished not only a splendid portrait but has revealed the living realisation of a typical Scottish intellectual…Mr. Baird…is a staunch supporter of the Celtic art renaissance that is dawning after a period of hibernation.[8]

It seems that the portrait, together with MacColla's novel, was the fruit of a close creative partnership between the two men. MacColla would have sat for hours for Baird's portrait. Baird, in his turn, signed official legal papers relating to the publication of *The Albannach* and is likely to have read the draft at various stages. *The Albannach* appeared shortly after Baird's portrait to equally favourable reviews. Writing in the *Modern Scot*, Edwin Muir acknowledged its 'undisciplined power…the making of a writer of the first class'.[9] For his part Hugh MacDiarmid lauded *The Albannach* as the best representation of the contemporary Gael in Scottish literature.

At the time of the London exhibition of *Portrait of a Young Scotsman* Baird gave his first significant interview to the press, a detailed discussion of the motivations behind the portrait with *The Angus and Mearns Herald*:

> It is an attempt to paint a modern and distinctively Scottish portrait…to make a synthesis between an acquired technique, partly from sources, an actively involved sense of being part of a re-vivified Scottish Culture, and lastly the individual and the model…He felt that Scots art wanted to make a new start, because the national idioms of Scots art had been overlaid by the false products of the 'kailyard' school, or its equivalent in art…The Italian primitives and the French School showed the way to develop an art which was characteristically Scottish.[10]

The intellectual debt to the Scottish Renaissance movement could not be more explicit. Baird dismisses the kailyard as 'false' and instead calls for a 're-vivified' Scottish culture engaging with the European mainstream - in particular France and Italy. This mention of French modernism is interesting as it is the first concrete evidence we have of Baird looking closely at the work of Matisse and Picasso and the classicising 'Call to Order' period of the 1920s. The lessons of the sojourn in Italy were clearly still prominent in his thoughts. In his call for a 'true' Scottish culture, Baird here seems to mediate between the claims of French modernism and Italian classicism, at the same time insisting on the need for art to reflect contemporary life, particularly in the representation of his close relationship with 'the model', MacColla. The portrait self-consciously elevated MacColla to the ranks of a new generation of emergent Renaissance intellectuals.

When *Portrait of a Young Scotsman* was exhibited at the Royal Scottish Academy in Edinburgh in 1933, it received further favourable press comment. The most qualified of the reviews, perhaps surprisingly, came from James H. Whyte in the pages of his cultural journal, *Modern Scot*:

> A picture which would undoubtedly stand out if it were not almost killed by a big frame of mirror glass just beside it, is Edward McEwan Baird's *Portrait of a Young Scotsman*. There is no finer draughtsman in the exhibition than Mr Baird, but his colour scheme is rather insipid, being superimposed like a wash on the drawing.[11]

Whyte outlines a recurring criticism of Baird's work - an over-concentration on draughtsmanship and composition at the expense of other aspects of the painting. In some paintings - particularly the sketches that were never translated into larger works - the battle for dominance between the painterly 'idea' and its realisation is striking. However, despite his reservations, Whyte bought the painting after the RSA exhibition for an undisclosed sum and it entered his personal collection in St. Andrews. The painting re-appeared in an exhibition organised by Whyte in the summer of 1935 in his North Street gallery, after which it spent a period on loan at the Edinburgh headquarters of the SNP.

It has been commonly assumed that *Portrait of a Young Scotsman* returned to the USA with Whyte in 1940, but a check with his relatives has drawn a blank. It is possible, but unlikely, that Whyte may have sold the painting to a private collector from his gallery in Washington D.C. after World War II. Unfortunately, the likelier scenario is that the portrait remained in Scotland with Whyte's then partner, the art critic, John Tonge, and that following the latter's death in the 1950s it was thrown away when his house was cleared. Given the interest of the media in this image and the importance that Baird attached to it as an early expression of his commitment to the ideas of the Scottish Renaissance, this is a real loss. The disappearance and possible ignominious demise of this key portrait is sadly all too typical of the fate of some of Baird's paintings.

Fortunately another portrait from this period survives, that of Allan Ogilvie's wife, Susan. *Mrs Ogilvie* (41) also dates to 1932 and it is likely that Baird worked on this portrait contemporaneously with *Portrait of a Young Scotsman*. The Ogilvies had married in 1928 and it is likely that it was commissioned sometime after Baird's return to Montrose. Ogilvie had a lifelong interest in the arts and was naturally garrulous; such a friendship was of obvious value to the artist.

The portraits of a close friend and of the wife of a close friend show that Baird preferred to draw his subjects from his immediate circle at this time. His life seems to have been at its fullest socially during this period, as he had become engaged to Ann Fairweather in 1931. A contemporary photograph shows a happy-looking Baird and a fashionably dressed Ann, standing next to a joke snow sculpture at Montrose harbour. Baird and Ann are remembered as good and interesting company, each possessed of a bitingly dry sense of humour, which occasionally boiled over into fierce arguments. Baird's relationship with Ann was to prove critically important in the difficult years after the 1930s depression and during the war. As his career developed, Ann appears more frequently as a model in his paintings.

Mrs Ogilvie is an unusual portrait. Born Susan Rachel Fergusson in 1903 on the remote island of St. Kilda, west of the Outer Hebrides, she had been evacuated from the island sometime during the First World War and had spent the remainder of her childhood in Aberdeen. In 1930 the final thirty-six inhabitants were evacuated from St. Kilda, allowing a romanticised myth of 'abandoned St. Kilda' to grow in the Scottish media. Posters advertising ferries and day trips to 'lonely St. Kilda' appeared as the decade wore on.[12] Baird would have taken an interest in this unusual story and that would have been sharpened by a talk that he attended on the subject of St. Kilda, given in Montrose by Ogilvie's father-in-law during the summer of 1932. As Baird never visited the island, it seems that a combination of this public lecture, conversations with the Ogilvies and contemporary newspaper and magazine accounts informed his composition.

Susan Ogilvie is foregrounded, in semi-profile, looking over the left shoulder of the spectator. This is a deft compositional device as it enables us to see more of Baird's imagined St. Kilda landscape behind. She is depicted looking rather formal, her features set in contemplation, her hair tied in a severe bun. The muted blue of her blouse gives way to the visceral greens and browns of the landscape behind and the grey-blue of an animated sea and lowering sky. Baird's depiction of St. Kilda is actually quite realistic, save for the isolated white-painted cottages and stone wall,

41 MRS OGILVIE

which perhaps owe more to contemporary depictions of Cornwall. Perhaps the contemplative appearance of Mrs Ogilvie reflects the nature of their conversations during her sitting for the portrait, as she remembered a past way of life gone forever.

Baird was to see a good deal of the Ogilvies and other friends in the NPS at this time, as a parliamentary by-election took place in the town in June-July 1932 following the elevation of the sitting member to the House of Lords. Montrose, though nowadays part of the staunchly Scottish Nationalist heartland of Angus, was then a Liberal town and the local press held out little hope for a successful NPS campaign. Independent Labour Party and Liberal opponents filled the correspondence columns of the *Montrose Review* in advance of the campaign with a rubbishing of the new party's credentials. A staff journalist at the paper underlined the seeming hopelessness of the nationalist cause, writing 'It is unlikely that they will put forward a candidate. The NPS has practically no organisation whatever in the Burghs, and it would be a forlorn fight on their part'.[13]

This pessimistic assessment shows that the NPS was largely confined to the ranks of Baird's friends within the town itself. Despite this, however, the NPS did field a candidate in Douglas Elmslie. MacColla returned to Montrose to help with the campaign and it seems likely that Baird was involved himself alongside Allan Ogilvie, Peter Machir, Andrew Dalgetty and the architect, George Fairweather. Predictably, Elmslie finished bottom of the poll as the Liberal candidate triumphed, but he garnered nearly 2,000 votes and, at 11% of the vote, this was a good result for a newly-formed party with few members, no money and little profile. It certainly was a better showing than the callow farce of the by-election in East Fife the following year. Here the nationalists, backed by MacDiarmid and Whyte, were humiliated by financial misfortune and low support in a campaign laden with such rich comic potential that it was satirised in Eric Linklater's celebrated novel, *Magnus Merriman*, published in 1935.

This was to be the last explicit involvement Baird had with active electoral politics. Following this by-election the local branch seems to have imploded in petty squabbling with national headquarters in Edinburgh. The reasons for this remain obscure and not even the emollient Allan Ogilvie could find a solution. Ultimately this in-fighting was subsumed by the NPS's merger with the Duke of Montrose's right wing, monarchical Scottish Party in 1934 to produce the present day Scottish National Party. The SNP spent the run-up to the war in in-fighting and expelling the more extreme cultural fringe in its ranks, including MacDiarmid. Baird, like so many others, seems to have drifted away and, as we shall see in the next chapter, had moved towards a position of communitarian socialism by the outbreak of war.

Despite these growing doubts about political nationalism, Baird remained fiercely committed to the re-emergence of an avowedly Scottish culture in his art. His next commissioned portrait, *William McCausland Stewart* (45), was probably brought about through the intervention of Whyte. Stewart was a Lecturer in French at the University of St. Andrews in the 1930s and lived next door to the Muirs in the town's South Street. Through this proximity to the Muirs he found himself on the fringes of the Scottish Renaissance grouping. It is likely that Baird visited St. Andrews to paint the academic over several sittings. A small surviving reproduction of the work shows Stewart seated in a similar semi-profile pose to Susan Ogilvie. In the background are the forms of his study and a severely geometricised bookshelf, suggesting that this portrait was another attempt to build up an impression of the depth and variety of thinker associated with the Renaissance. After the war Stewart had a distinguished career as Professor of French at the University of Bristol. He still had the portrait with him at his death sometime in the early 1990s. The author was unable to trace his surviving family during research for this book, although it is assumed that the work remains with them.

1933 also saw Baird engaged in an unusual portrait of local Montrose choirboy, Iain Pirie. We do not have any details of Pirie or how the painting came about. This image marks the beginnings of a move away from portraits laden with cultural politics, such as *Portrait of a Young Scotsman* or *Mrs Ogilvie*, towards a series of paintings exploring the community in Montrose through portrait and townscape. *Choir Boy (Iain Pirie)* (44) is an acutely observed figure study. The boy is shown in his robes against a neutral brown background. In contrast to the active contemplation of Susan Ogilvie in her portrait, Pirie is shown as almost frozen in the gaze of the artist, perhaps reflecting his nervousness at being asked to sit still for long and unforgiving hours. Rather oddly, there is an unspecified geometric form by the sitter's left shoulder. It is possible that this may be some form of tribal mask or carving, but it is impossible to be sure. This form, emerging from the neutral background, has an uncomfortable relationship with the sitter and looks forward to similarly complex spatial relationships in later paintings such as *Unidentified Aircraft* and *Angus and Mearns*. This geometric passage may also give an indication of the restlessness of Baird's mind. Frequently, whilst concentrating hard on completing one image, Baird would think ahead to future canvases. On the back of different canvases Baird jotted down ideas for future work, such as a list of native American tribes or a rough cross-section of a human eyeball with various optical notations. Despite his passionate interest in the history of native American tribes and optics, Baird never completed an image with either as its subject. For all his prodigious powers of

47 BIRTH OF VENUS

concentration and meticulous attention to detail, these notations provide an interesting insight into an ambitious and wide-ranging intellect.

Although Baird was increasingly turning towards the people and places of Montrose for subject matter, his next work was a very personal one. In 1934 his old friend, James McIntosh Patrick, married and Baird acted as best man. As a wedding present he completed one of his best known images, *Birth of Venus*, which, typically, he did not regard as properly finished until the following autumn. *Birth of Venus* encompasses all of the interests in art that Baird and McIntosh Patrick had in common and for that reason stands as a touching tribute to the closeness of their friendship. The painting clearly refers to Sandro Botticelli's canonical image of the same name, painted around 1485 and now part of the Uffizi collection in Florence. It is very probable that Baird saw Botticelli's painting during his visit to Florence in April-May 1929. As with Botticelli, Baird depicts a nude female figure at the centre of the painting, emerging from the waves, bounded on either side by a detailed jumble of still life objects, including shells, marine flora and fauna, navigational aids, markers and buoys. The colouration is very well controlled. The eye is automatically drawn to the standing nude at the centre, then drops down across the sand, coming to rest in the pale violet of the fern. This in turn gives way to the greys and mauves of the shells to the left and the beautifully-observed patterned textures of wood, terminating in the final simmering black of the navigational aids. The jewel-like clarity of the colours echoes the temperas of the Italian 'primitive' artists.

This image is distinctively a Scottish one. The beach is Montrose with Baird depicting a becalmed North Sea and huge clear sky in the background. The female figure is Ann Fairweather. Significantly, this was the first nude image of Ann that Baird had completed; several more were to follow. The chosen still-life elements are interesting. The groups of large shells to the bottom left are oversized and imply an overt sexuality. Above, a complex pattern of mirrors and navigational devices adds a contemporary reference to this timeless, idealised composition. The exotic marine fern, painted in 'Marsh Violet' and pushed up against the picture plane, echoes the upright, stretching pose of the nude behind. We have already noted the link between the upright shell to the right of the fern to Baird's earliest still-life drawings at Montrose Academy. On the extreme right a depiction of a plaster bust sits awkwardly in relation to the rest of the image. Here Baird carries on his experimentation with pictorial space suggested in *Choir Boy*. Perhaps the bust was included as a humourous reference to the many hours that Baird and McIntosh Patrick spent drawing in still-life classes at art school. The mood of the painting is not entirely serious. The letters 'E.N.I.T.' underneath the right-hand fern leaf stand for a personal joke between Baird and McIntosh Patrick, the precise details of which are now lost.[14]

These light-hearted touches do not take away from the fact that this was as concentrated an image of love that Baird was capable of producing at this time. *Birth of Venus* includes the woman he was to marry, his love of the sea and of sailing and Montrose beach and the North Sea at its calmest, places where he had spent much leisure time from childhood. The still-life objects fulfil both symbolic functions in building up a narrative of love and also a nostalgic look back at his development as an artist from his schooldays. Rooted in the artist's deep admiration for the work of the Italian 'primitives' and Botticelli, *Birth of Venus* stands as an avowedly contemporary summary of Baird's vision to that date, the importance of McIntosh Patrick in that process and his hopes for a happily married future for his friend. Knowing that Baird very rarely parted with his paintings, McIntosh Patrick was very touched by the gift, as his memoir makes clear.[15]

However McIntosh Patrick probably misjudged the importance of the English painter, Edward Wadsworth (1889-1949), for this work. Wadsworth spent the later 1920s and 1930s painting marine still-lifes. Wadsworth's work developed in parallel with continental surrealism and abstraction and during the 1920s he was one of the very few contemporary English artists taken seriously by critics and collectors on the Continent. In the UK Wadsworth exhibited regularly and his work was frequently reproduced in art magazines.[16]

A typical Wadsworth image of the period is *Regalia*, completed in 1928 and now in the collection of Tate Britain in London. Wadsworth's method would have interested Baird, as the Englishman also experimented at length with egg tempera and oils. In *Regalia* the picture is dominated by a table-top still-life jumble of modern nautical equipment, nets and shells, with a calm sea and sky behind. However in no way should a direct link between *Regalia* and *Birth of Venus* be assumed. It is likely that Baird knew Wadsworth's work and was interested in it for its subject matter and technique. Similarly, the painting is sometimes cited as evidence of Baird's affinity with 'Surrealism'. Again the artist would have known of Surrealism and its ideas, but he is unlikely to have embraced them with any enthusiasm. As we shall see in the next chapter, Baird seems to have had a pragmatic approach to the work of contemporaries. In the idiom of Wadsworth he may have found part of the answer to the complex compositional problems posed in the completion of his painting, even if he remained sceptical of some of the theoretical 'justifications' that sometimes accompanied his work.

McIntosh Patrick's memoir shows that Baird experienced protracted technical difficulties in the completion of this work, as the red underpainting kept showing through the final oil glaze.

(LEFT) Sandro Botticelli (c.1445-1510) THE BIRTH OF VENUS
(RIGHT) Edward Wadsworth (1889-1949) REGALIA 1928 (Tate Britain)

This, and the final painting of the 'Marsh Violet' marine fern, meant that Baird did not deliver *Birth of Venus* to his friend's house in Dundee until late 1935. Baird worked over the colours and added small details throughout the year. The painting was exhibited at a show organised by George Cathro in Montrose in September of the same year. *Birth of Venus* must have looked incongruous, shown alongside the work of amateur and semi-professional artists working in traditional styles. Surprisingly this was the only time that Baird contributed to one of Cathro's exhibitions. The painting created quite a puzzled reaction in the local press. The reviewer of the *Montrose Standard* noted 'This is in the type of the school of Surrealism, and supporters of this school will recognise its beauty and splendid detail',[17] whilst the *Montrose Review* suggested that the work was '…a departure from the conventional…it is not a problem picture, but to some it may be rather difficult to understand. This, unfortunately, is the only example of Mr. Baird's work'.[18] *Birth of Venus* was the first 'Surrealist' and 'Modernist' work ever shown in Montrose, which may account for these rather hesitant responses. The painting also caused some local scandal and embarrassment for its depiction of Ann Fairweather in the nude. After this exhibition the painting moved to Dundee, but was kept by Baird for safekeeping in Montrose during the war, whilst McIntosh Patrick served in the army.[19]

By the end of 1935 the Scottish Renaissance was on the verge of petering out in St. Andrews and was a fading memory in Montrose.[20] Nonetheless it had had an invigorating effect on Baird's art and had offered a credible post-art school direction for him to follow. The success of works such as *Portrait of a Young Scotsman* and *Birth of Venus* had shown that it was possible to relate to international modernism in an idiom that took account of early Renaissance influences, whilst remaining grounded in a specifically local vernacular. Baird's decision to return to Montrose after his studies, which some may have regarded as an eccentric choice in the development of an artistic career, had paid off with the development of connections in avant-garde circles in art, and in the newest political party then active in Scotland. As the 1930s wore on Baird was to apply his highly politicised view of art in the representation of the places and communities of Montrose. With the waning of his friends' influence in art and politics in the second half of the decade, he was ever more reliant on close friends and family for support, encouragement and subject matter. During this process he had also to fully reconcile his views on contemporary modernism. It is to this debate that we now turn.

EDWARD BAIRD
AND ANN
WITH A SNOW
SCULPTURE

4. 'DISTRESSED AREA': BAIRD AND MODERNISM

Sometime after handing over *Birth of Venus* to James McIntosh Patrick, Baird rented his first studio at 3a Bridge Street in Montrose. Space at his mother's house in the High Street is likely to have become restricted as the number of canvases in preparation - and finished - grew. Together with the need to have a separate space in which to paint and the amount of room that his materials and easel took up, this was a practical solution. It is uncertain how Baird afforded the rent for his studio or, indeed, lived from day to day. When money earned from painting ran out, it is probable that his mother intervened. A letter from Allan Ogilvie in Montrose Museum's archive states that Baird's mother provided for his meals, cigarettes and accommodation throughout this period.[1] Baird is likely to have paid for his studio from the small amount of money earned from paintings sold. It must have been a precarious and constrained existence, although, given his slow pace of work and frequent ill-health, it is difficult to see how it could have been otherwise. The artist's only steady income over this period came from his job as a visiting lecturer at Dundee College of Art, where he was employed from 1938 to 1940.

As the Scottish Renaissance ran out of steam, Baird's circle of friends altered. He lost contact with Whyte in the second half of the 1930s and MacColla moved permanently away from Montrose, first to Edinburgh and then later to Letterfourie in Banffshire in 1938.[2] Increasingly Baird spent time with his future brother-in-law and close friend, the architect George Fairweather (1906-86). Apocryphal tales abound from this period of Baird and other nationalists, including Peter Machir, Andrew Dalgetty and Allan Ogilvie, gathering at Fairweather's premises in the High Street of an evening and setting the world to rights. It was probably also around this time that Baird saw the Montrose sculptor, William Lamb. However the relationship was never close. Lamb did sculpt a portrait bust of Baird that probably dates to the mid 1930s, which, given the sculptor's rapid modelling style, probably took no more than a couple of sessions to complete at Lamb's studio in Market Street. However, as Jake Stewart has noted, Fairweather seems to have preferred to keep the two artists apart from one another:

> Although Lamb and Baird held a mutual respect for each other's work, the relationship between the artists can be summed up as cool with heated periods. George Fairweather was fond of both Lamb and Baird, but appears to have done his best to keep them apart.[3]

Baird worked closely with Fairweather in the mid-1930s. By this stage Fairweather was an

50 WALTER GRAHAM

established architect with offices in Montrose and London. He was noted locally for his Art Deco construction by Montrose beach, which still stands to this day. Baird and Fairweather collaborated on other schemes. In a drawing entitled 'Carving in Plaster', completed in red crayon, Baird envisages the interior decorations in a plan for a proposed cinema designed by Fairweather. These are wonderful relief-style designs of female muses, groups of musicians, musical instruments, with at the top of the drawing a personification of drama overseeing all. Sadly the plan did not progress beyond the drawing board, but provides evidence of a fertile creative relationship between the two men in the mid 1930s.

The first portrait Baird completed in his new Bridge Street studio was of Fairweather. A photograph of Fairweather posing for his portrait still exists and it is likely that Baird would have worked from this in addition to formal sittings with his subject. As a busy professional, Fairweather is unlikely to have had the time to subject himself to the gruelling sittings that Baird required to produce portraits. *George Fairweather* FRIBA (48) shows the architect seated at his drawing board, wearing his working smock. In addition to providing a typically meticulous impression of Fairweather's appearance, Baird uses the props of the architect's trade: drawing board, set square, rulers and rolled up plans. It seems that Baird has painted Fairweather's figure from the black and white photograph and added the desk and props separately from the architect's office. This probably accounts for the uneasy relationship between figure and still-life. The rulers and plans project out over the edge of the desk into the space occupied by the figure. It seems that Baird wants us to focus closely on the figure; there is little appeal to our sense of colour in a restricted palette of muted greens and greys. Baird exhibited the portrait at the Royal Scottish Academy in 1936, his work appearing for the first time since 1933. By this time the work was listed as belonging to Fairweather, so presumably the architect had purchased it sometime early that year.

By the time of the RSA exhibition Baird was working on his next studio portrait - his uncle and lifelong confidant, Walter Graham. Photographs from this period show Graham and Baird's Aunt Wilhelmina seated in the garden at Craig Hill with their pet wire-haired terrier dog. At the same time as painting Graham's portrait, Baird completed a small painting of this dog with a ball on Montrose beach, which stylistically seems to relate to the earlier *Birth of Venus*. The picture was never exhibited - it may have been intended as a present for his uncle - and it has long since disappeared.

As with the Fairweather portrait, Walter Graham's pose has been carefully staged. Another black and white photograph shows Graham sitting in the Bridge Street studio in front of the chessboard. Again Baird seems to have mixed formal sittings with use of the photograph. The sitter is shown as unaware of the spectator's presence, contemplating his next move in a chess game in which presumably Baird was his opponent. Graham's head has been painted with a particularly microscopic intensity. The effect of the detail is heightened as, in contrast to the Fairweather portrait, Baird has neglected to include any background detail. His uncle's face stands out clearly against the neutral coloured background. In terms of the picture's lighting - from above the spectator's right shoulder - Baird evokes the lighting of portraits by Henry Raeburn.

According to Patrick Elliott, Baird's technique in *Walter Graham* (50) self-consciously echoed those of early Netherlandish painters:

> Influenced by the technique of Flemish masters such as Van Eyck, Baird would first paint with a monochrome underbase and then layer it with glazes on top. If a white ground was used the paint could yellow with age and become transparent. This has happened in the Graham portrait where the re-worked chess pieces have almost disappeared…[4]

As with earlier works in tempera from the 1920s, the foreground of the portrait has now deteriorated terribly and the raw canvas is visible in several areas. This has affected the chessboard in particular and the area around the sitter's fingers. This problem has not affected subsequent portraits and, given the technical difficulties already experienced in the completion of *Birth of Venus*, it seems likely that Baird slightly altered his technique during or shortly after the completion of this work.

The portraits of Fairweather and Graham suggest a slightly altered direction for Baird. The explicitly political portraiture of the early 1930s has given way to a more studied focus on the methods and techniques of classical art. In both pictures Baird moves towards a tighter conception of traditional portraiture. As in the work of Raeburn or Ingres, the artist focuses on giving the spectator as thorough an understanding of the appearance of the sitter, concentrating on the hands and the eyes. Our understanding of the status of these sitters is augmented by Baird's use of props. We have already noted the architectural instruments present in *George Fairweather*. In *Walter Graham* the chessboard is used to underline the schoolmaster's status as a man of education, learning and wisdom.

This change in direction did not mark a retreat from his interest in politics, however. Rather it suggests an ongoing critique of the formal and theoretical articulation of modernism in the arts and, from that, a meditation on the role of the artist in society. Two pieces of evidence remain which relate to this process. The first is found in an unlikely place, a child's autograph book. During the author's research a small pastiche of a post-Cubist painting that Baird had drawn some time in the 1930s for a young girl called Helen Fulton was discovered. Titled *Modern <u>Art</u> a Long Way <u>after</u> poor Pablo and Henri* (42), this little sketch is a near-perfect lampooning of the imitation of modern French painting by British artists. Baird has broken up the picture into clashing, Cubist-style space. The word 'Piccasso' is (perhaps deliberately) mis-spelled in a collage-style use of lettering. The little picture is gaudily patterned and coloured in dominant yellows, blues and purples.

Whilst clearly this is a light-hearted sketch for a child, the ideas behind it would have been seriously held. We have already established that Baird developed a working knowledge of European modernism during his studies in Glasgow. McIntosh Patrick points out in his memoir that Baird's style was the antithesis of Maurice Greiffenhagen's exotic decorative idiom and ran counter to the Colourist interest in the work of Cézanne and the Fauves. This little sketch suggests that, whilst Baird would have been very interested in Matisse and Picasso's own work, he is likely to have been contemptuous of those British artists who sought to emulate them in a self-identifying 'modernist' strategy.

Firmer evidence of Baird's critical attitude towards discourses on modernism is found in the manuscript of a lecture given to the Dundee Art Society probably sometime during 1938-40. Entitled 'How Useful is Art', the lecture contrasts modernist painting with the art of the early Renaissance. As with everything else, Baird obviously spent a great deal of time choosing his words for the lecture, as the manuscript is scored with corrections and alterations. Baird longed for past times, when:

> ...art worked in blissful ignorance of its own nature. It believed it was only a trick in the amusement and service of mankind, and existed to paint flowers to deceive bees, to celebrate feats of arms, to adorn council chambers, to charm away melancholy and to teach and improve the people.[5]

Two themes emerge here. First, there is a desire for art to be less self-conscious and less concerned with critical legitimisation and aimed more at being relevant to its audience by delighting and entertaining them. There is also, in Baird's prescription, a clear didactic role for painting, a view that very few of his contemporaries would have shared. After all this was an idea that had not been taken seriously since Edwardian times. Second, Baird seems to hold a strongly-idealised view of the early Italian Renaissance. The model he outlines of the artist-as-craftsman 'serving' society, rather than living 'apart' from society in the rarefied sphere of aesthetics or celebrity, echoes strongly the role of the Renaissance artist as 'serving' a patron, and earning recognition from a wider community for that patron through the beauty of his work.

Baird contrasts this ideal state with the bewildering multiplicity of theories employed as justification of non-representational art in the 1930s:

This living by itself combined with its awakened self consciousness has produced a strange crop of ideas and theories with which Art torments itself…It is a great churning sea of words in which fragments of reasoning torn from who can say what source roll ceaseless about the waves in incessant collision with each other, and solid lumps of unexamined statement and under-defined terms appear again and again, monotonously, amongst the foam.[6]

Baird's impatience with contemporary criticism and art theory is made very plain through his extended marine metaphor. This passage appears at the end of a long, adjective-heavy savaging of modernist discourse as a whole. As with many practising artists, Baird's contempt for the 'critic' is heartfelt. He is suggesting here that the critic has only become necessary owing to modernism's deviation away from the 'true' purpose of art. Indeed Baird has much to say on the subject of 'truth' in art:

Truth is just as fierce a master as Art and will not be played with, with impunity…Art in this crystalline world of reason is but part of a totality which is the whole of human activity: among these activities it has, regardless of the critics and the wishes of artists, an immutable position determined by truth itself.[7]

For Baird 'art' and 'truth' are two sides of the same coin. The artist must not only make his subject matter intelligible to various different audience groups within the community, he must not flinch from reflecting the true nature of the subject represented. Here we see a plea for contemporary art to be politically as well as aesthetically engaged. Art is an activity of the 'practical intellect' and hence is one tool amongst many for speculation on, and analysis of, the society which produced it.

This point of view is a decisive rejection of 'art for art's sake' and the critical positions that went with it. Holding such views, we can now see why Baird was so quick to lampoon the pleasant, unchallenging Francophile echoes of the Bloomsbury and London groups of the 1920s and the work of abstract artists in the 1930s. Non-representational artists, such as Ben Nicholson, Barbara Hepworth and Naum Gabo, sought to find a set of ideal relationships in their work in an attempt to lead society towards the better. Baird refused the luxury of such metaphysical speculation. For him the artist was a practical craftsman serving society alongside the joiner or the skilled agricultural labourer. These reflections were not uncritical, however, as it was the duty of the artist to pass comment on society as he found it in the highly moral pursuit of the ideal of 'truth'.

It would be easy to dismiss Baird as an arch-conservative on the basis of the 'How Useful is Art?' manuscript. In the author's view such an assessment misses the point entirely. The artist does not issue any Alfred Munnings-style call for artists to 'paint skies better', but merely expresses frustration at what he sees as the vacuity and irrelevance of modernist practice to the vast majority

Meredith Frampton (1894-1984)
MARGUERITE KELSEY 1928 (Tate Britain)

of the public. In many ways Baird's call for a realist, socially-engaged art parallels the ideas of the Socialist Realist painters or the Euston Road School in the second half of the 1930s.

Yet idiomatically he is different from both those groups of artists. The closest equivalent to Baird's style at this time was the academic portraitist, Meredith Frampton, whose work Baird would have seen at the annual Royal Academy exhibitions at Burlington House. Frampton's uncompromisingly neo-classical portraits of fashionable women, such as the 1928 canvas *Marguerite Kelsey* (Tate Britain), relate to Baird's work in terms of their restricted palette, elegant composition and tight control of spatial relations. Although the artists were contemporaries, there is no evidence of them ever having met. Nonetheless, it is tempting to view both Baird's Renaissance portraits and his depiction of close friends such as Fairweather and Graham as an attempt to re-kindle a kind of Scottish classicism, set apart from the theoretical relativism of contemporary modern painting. Given the strong idealising passages about the role of the artist as craftsman, it is not too fanciful to suggest that Baird saw himself as Montrose's 'artist', reflecting and serving the community he knew so well.

Baird's profile was raised in 1936 by the illustration of *George Fairweather* in a special number of *The Studio* devoted to Scottish Art.[8] Baird was recognised by a reviewer as running against the grain of contemporary painting:

For some people (states a critic) Mr Baird's handling of *George Fairweather*, formerly of Montrose and now of London, is maybe a little 'too tight'. It is one of the most outstanding of recent Scots portraits, however. Mr Baird does not shake pictures out of his sleeve like your fashionable Chelsea juggler, and months of painstaking work has gone into this beautifully composed picture.[9]

Baird here is identified as a significant contributor to modern Scottish painting, making that contribution from an unusual perspective. More and more he was to offer in his paintings from c.1936-39 a social critique of an increasingly polarised society.

Baird began to see less of Fairweather from 1936 onwards as the architect began to spend more time in London. During this period he began to socialise more with itinerant workers and labourers at Montrose Harbour, including the fisherman and labourer, Alicky Brannan, and the poacher, James 'Pumphy' Davidson. Sometime around this period Peter Machir returned from a spell working in England, where he had been badly injured in an industrial accident. Machir was confined largely to his house in Wharf Street, near to Brannan's dilapidated dwelling, and was unable to work seriously again. Baird's kindness and support towards his old friend is still remembered by Machir's family.

By 1936 the effects of the global economic depression were being felt keenly in Montrose. The pages of the local papers are filled with gloomy statistics of the men claiming means-tested support at the Montrose Labour Exchange. Many came from outside Montrose to look for work in seasonal tourist trades and competition for jobs in the more stable sectors of light industry and agriculture was fierce. The influx of people to Montrose seeking employment affected all aspects of life in the town. By the late 1930s Montrose's semi-professional football team was made up almost entirely of itinerant Glaswegian players.[10]

Towards the end of 1936 Baird began work on a canvas called *Distressed Area* (51). It is likely that he took the title of the work from a book by the nationalist economic commentator, George Malcolm Thompson. In *Scotland: That Distressed Area* Thompson offers a damning critique of the National Government's economic policies and their impact on Scotland, which, in Thompson's view, were particularly severe. Intriguingly, too, Thompson holds out little prospect of the SNP being able to develop credible solutions to these problems:

> The intellectual foundations of the party would evidently be strengthened if it be shown that its appeal is not based solely on national culture and traditions, but can equip itself with political weapons from the arsenal of economic interest.[11]

Thompson's impatience with the failure of the SNP to develop credible solutions to Scotland's recession is likely to have been shared by Baird. In *Distressed Area* we can see an indictment of the effects of the recession in Montrose and a subtle shift in his political views.

51 DISTRESSED AREA

Distressed Area has as its focus the boating shed of Alicky Brannan, situated on Rossie Island in the River Esk. The shed is closed up, disused tools are propped up against its outer wall and the long grass and scarlet weeds in the foreground give the impression of disuse and decay. In the background both Montrose harbour and the fishing village of Ferryden on the south bank of the Esk are shown; no activity of any sort is discernible. The harbour lies deserted, unvisited by shipping of any kind. On the opposite side of the river Ferryden's dwindling fishing fleet lies at anchor. Only some washing hanging on a line by the water's edge gives some indication of a continuing human presence.

The painting is imbued with an atmosphere of unnatural calm and long-term inactivity. *Distressed Area* follows Baird's own prescription for a Scottish classicism thoroughly engaged with contemporary issues. The spectator can simply enjoy the care with which Baird has represented an unusual perspective on both Montrose and Ferryden. The inactivity, however, would not have been lost on contemporary audiences. It is an eloquent indictment of the impact that failed economic management has on the lives of ordinary people, completed in a subtle and understated manner. It is a theme that recurs in Scottish writing in the 1930s. This powerful portrayal of idleness and decay echoes the depiction of unemployment in Grassic Gibbon's *Grey Granite* and in the final chapters of Barke's *The Land of the Leal*, set in depression-hit Glasgow.

Distressed Area also had deep personal significance for Baird. We know anecdotally that both he and George Fairweather had built the boating shed for Brannan and there has been a suggestion that Baird occasionally used the space as a studio. Baird's small boat is also likely to have been kept at the shed. Contemporary photographs show Baird and a party of friends, including Ann Fairweather and Tom Whiston, sailing across the Esk to Ferryden. Patrick Elliott and others also have suggested that Baird and Fairweather intended the shed to be the first building of an artists' and workers' settlement on Rossie Island, plans that seem to have been shelved with Fairweather spending more and more time at his practice in London.[12]

It was at about this time that Baird seems to have become involved with the Workers' Education Association in Montrose. The WEA was a charitable and philanthropic organisation that sought to provide practical relief in terms of food and entertainment to unemployed workers. This is clear evidence of Baird become frustrated with the failure of political nationalism and desiring to help those struggling as a result of casual employment or joblessness. The boating hut was used as an occasional venue for WEA meetings and in wartime as a space for Christmas parties for local children.[13] Thus began Baird's involvement in practical community-based organisations that, as we shall see in the next chapter, peaked during World War II.

Baird worked on *Distressed Area* between 1936 and 1938 and exhibited the painting that summer at the Royal Scottish Academy. During these years he began to experiment with watercolour. One such watercolour, *The Fifie* (49), painted at Montrose harbour in just one day in 1936, represents another political intervention from the artist. At first glance *The Fifie* appears to be a straightforward representation of a fishing boat tied up at Montrose harbour, albeit seen from an unusual angled perspective. However in a detailed letter to Fairweather Baird explained the motivation behind his painting:

> My excuse for making such a documentary drawing of the fishing boat is that it is a type with a history which with the wanton destruction of the inshore fishing industry is likely to come to a close.[14]

Here, the artist identifies another function of his art, existing in tandem with his formal studio painting, namely, the idea of the commemorative 'documentary' image. The 'Fifie' was one of the first three rough water sailing boats in the world, designed to withstand the caprices of the North Sea during longer than usual voyages. In this sense Baird's painting functions both as a historical representation of a disappearing pattern of work and an implicit criticism of the policies leading to its demise. As Baird was spending much time at the harbour in the late 1930s, he would have been keenly aware of the effect of these policies on the living of the fishermen he would have seen on an almost daily basis. This 'documentary' function is another link between Baird and the Euston Road School, whose ideas in part were to coalesce in the 'Mass Observation' project during World War II.

Another descriptive watercolour from this period survives, dating from 1938. *High Street, Montrose* (54) is sketched from a vantage point of some 150 yards south-west of the Auld Kirk, just outside Baird's studio at 3a Bridge Street. The sketching again appears to have been done rapidly. The image is more an experimentation with lively colours than fulfilling a serious documentary function. Provost Butchart of Montrose bought the picture shortly after it was completed and it hung for a while in the town hall. It is likely that Baird would have received a guinea for this watercolour. He mentioned to Fairweather that he was completing paintings around this time that were 'not works of art', charging '£15 for an unframed landscape, and 25 shillings [£1.25] for drawings'.[15] No details - appearance, production or whereabouts - survive of these 'commissions'.

Two major studio projects occupied Baird's time in the last years of peace. Sometime in 1937 he began a large scale portrait of James 'Pumphy' Davidson. Baird had known Davidson since the early 1920s and the work was provisionally entitled 'The Gamekeeper'. This title is likely to have

55 MONROS

been an in-joke, as Davidson was a notorious poacher, who frequently sailed very close to the breeze in terms of prosecution. The painting developed through Baird's by now established method of formal sittings and painting after photographs. In a later media interview Davidson remembered these sittings as particularly demanding: 'I had to sit very still so as not to put him off'.[16] The portrait was the largest in scale yet attempted by Baird. A photograph of the work in progress shows that the artist had roughed out the figure in red chalk or crayon before painting directly in oils on top of this outline. The progress of the painting was delayed considerably by the presence of Davidson's Black Labrador puppy. Not surprisingly the creature would not sit still for Baird and eventually had to be photographed and added at a late stage. This photograph of the puppy also resulted in a separate pastel and charcoal sketch.

In its original conception 'The Gamekeeper' sought to present Davidson as the embodiment of a Scottish rural labourer. We see the sitter as a man who works on the land, but whose character is also synonymous with his surroundings. The composition of the portrait leaves us with the impression that Davidson is emblematic of the more distant landscape behind. At first glance this is an idealised, depopulated landscape. Yet the figure of Davidson shows us that, for all its beauty, the countryside of Angus was still a working area with a significant economic contribution to make, rather than a passive spectacle of tourist beauty. This rural landscape was altered considerably - with much of the detail obliterated - by the time the painting was completed and, as we shall see, the whole context in which the image was seen changed fundamentally.

Alongside his slow and methodical work on 'The Gamekeeper', Baird returned to producing a composite nocturnal image of Montrose, entitled *Monros* (55), during 1937-39. This rather unusual small painting forms a link between the student drawing and tempera, *Figure Composition with Montrose Behind*, and the wartime canvas, *Unidentified Aircraft*. Baird returns to the Montrose of his memory with the old suspension bridge visible at the extreme left of the painting. That this is a painting of a past Montrose is evidenced by Baird's self-conscious use of an old vernacular name for the town in the title. The buildings, with the Auld Kirk dominating at the centre, press in on one another. The boats in the harbour and the fields in the foreground lie silent in the stillness of the night. It is possible to read this as a commemorative image, a nostalgic view of an old Montrose that had subtly faded away under the pressures of modernity. Baird's knowledge of, and interest in, the history of Montrose was commented on by a contemporary reviewer, noting 'A small painting this [Monros], but full of the personality of the artist'.[17]

Monros was exhibited alongside *Distressed Area* at the last peacetime show at the Royal Scottish Academy in Edinburgh in early summer 1939. Yet, although Baird had exhibited annually at the RSA from 1936, he had trouble maintaining any sort of profile or recognition from the art press from a provincial base. A reviewer of the 1938 RSA show, at which Baird exhibited *Distressed Area* and *High Street, Montrose*, seemed unaware that he was a consistent exhibitor:

> The 'discovery' of the exhibition is Edward Baird, who lives in the North and has not exhibited for some years. His 'Montrose' and 'Distressed Area' are amongst the best pictures in the show: the latter has none of the political or sociological bias its title might connote, but stands purely by the subtlety of the painting.[18]

The review's author speaks of 'the North' as though Baird lived in some remote, frozen wasteland and his refusal to engage with the political issues in *Distressed Area* is likely to stem from a similarly genuine ignorance of the effects that the depression had in provincial Scotland. The fact that the reviewer regards a painter established for nearly a decade as an important 'discovery' is also telling in regard to the painter's comparative obscurity outside Angus at this time.

The second half of the 1930s marked a series of important personal and professional developments for Baird. He had moved beyond the naïve optimism of his involvement with the Scottish Renaissance and political nationalism. He had reconciled the Renaissance's call for a re-invigorated Scottish culture, comfortable in the modern age, with his earlier interests in the Italian 'primitive' painters and the European classical tradition. This also allowed him to develop a cogent critique of contemporary modernist practice. His classical and culturally specific vision was given a vital cutting edge by his insistence on viewing art as part of, rather than apart from, the daily life of his community. In his sensitive and insightful studio portraits and in his painting of *Distressed Area* and *Monros*, Baird suggested a role for art as reflective of, and sympathetic to, the problems faced by ordinary people. This avowedly political engagement is also seen in documentary paintings, such as *The Fifie*.

Baird was not to know it, but, as war was declared in September 1939, these subtle shifts in intellectual outlook and a growing commitment to a neo-classical idiom were to provide him with a powerful basis from which to enter the most prolific and fulfilled years of his life.

5. AN ENGAGED VISION
1939-1944

Britain's declaration of war on Germany on 3rd September 1939 had immediate consequences. The atrocity of the bombing of Guernica in 1937 by aircraft of General Franco's Nationalist Air Force during the Spanish Civil War had given rise to general fears that major cities would be targeted by massed bomber formations. Air raid sirens sounded in many British cities immediately after Prime Minister Neville Chamberlain's broadcast, leading to a mood of fearful despondency and resignation amongst the civilian population.[1]

In the first three months of the war Montrose felt the effect of this fear of aerial attack. Some 2,500 civilians from Dundee had arrived in the town by December 1939, causing much friction and resentment in the local population. The lack of facilities for these incomers was aggravated by the unusually severe winter of 1939-40, when Montrose harbour froze over and coal and food rationing was introduced. The town also played host to an influx of RAF personnel. RAF Montrose had been recommissioned in December 1935 and in the early years of the war was worked up to a fully operational training base.[2]

Although much publicity surrounded the first German aircraft to be shot down over British soil in October 1939,[3] the massed bombing raids did not materialise and the incomers from Dundee began to return to their homes. Although the first months of the war were quickly dubbed the 'Phoney War', owing to a lack of sustained fighting, artists in the UK were not immune to having their lives irrevocably transformed by the war.[4]

The effects of wartime were felt in a number of ways. Many artists left London and other centres of the inter-war avant-garde for remote rural locations. Ben Nicholson, Barbara Hepworth and Naum Gabo left London in the last week of August 1939. Leading critic, Herbert Read, moved to Beaconsfield in Oxfordshire. Other artists, including Baird's old student friend, James McIntosh Patrick, joined the armed services.

Artists quickly found that the time and space they had to work in were severely restricted by the establishment of military exclusion zones, new wartime local defence duties and a sudden lack of materials. For example, many of Baird's favourite places around Montrose, such as areas of the beach and harbour and parts of the north end of the town surrounding the air base, were quickly designated off-limits for civilians. The availability of artists' materials diminished rapidly towards

56 LOCAL DEFENCE VOLUNTEER

the end of 1939 with oil paints and canvases almost unobtainable for a period as all production resources were switched to the war effort. Although Baird was exempt from all service - even in the newly-formed Local Defence Volunteers - on the grounds of ill health, other artists such as Ben Nicholson quickly found their working time eroded by military duties and the necessity to grow one's own food as rationing began to bite.[5] At the end of 1939 Kenneth Clark underlined the gravity of the conflict for artists in a radio discussion, noting 'painting has become, more than ever, an act of faith, a throwing of bread upon the waters, and only an artist with a strong creative impulse can continue undismayed'.[6]

In the early months of the war it quickly became apparent that visual art would have a vital role to play in chronicling the development of the war, responding to the events of the war in a documentary fashion and for the purposes of propaganda. In January 1940 the Royal Academy held an exhibition called 'United Artists', which, as its title suggests, saw the most advanced work of the avant-garde hung alongside paintings by conservative academicians in a show of cultural defiance in the face of prescriptive Fascist tyranny. Indeed art moved to centre stage as an important component of life on the 'home front'. The population's night-time movements were restricted by the blackout, so cultural activities such as readings, art appreciation and music were encouraged by the government. Arising partially from the success of the 'United Artists' exhibition, The Committee for the Encouragement of Music and the Arts was established in July 1940 to facilitate and co-ordinate cultural activity in wartime Britain. This was a democratic platform, which encouraged local artists, writers, musicians and cultural enthusiasts to organise exhibitions, reading, plays and concerts in their area. Soon a Montrose branch of CEMA was formed, which, as we shall see, provided an important local platform for Baird's work and views on art.

The outbreak of war was to have an immediate impact on Baird's *The Gamekeeper* as it neared completion. His sitter, James 'Pumphy' Davidson, was among the first men in Montrose to enlist in the newly-formed Local Defence Volunteers. Davidson arrived one morning at the Bridge Street studio proudly wearing his new LDV armband, which Baird immediately incorporated into his portrait. Baird shows Davidson seated with the black Labrador at his side, staring into the middle distance, set against the changed backdrop of the Angus hills and a lowering sky. As spectators we have a good idea of Davidson through the minute recording of his facial features and hands and his dress, with the checked jacket rather too neatly offset by a spotted neckerchief. Yet this is not an intimate portrait. The spectator is separated from Davidson's space by the rigid angle of the shotgun. Although the sitter looks over the head of the spectators, the dog gazes intently at us as though guarding against our intrusion.

These changed details profoundly altered the reception of the painting in 1940-1. Understandably the local and class issues of *Local Defence Volunteer* (LDV) (56) were superseded by the immediate context in which the picture was seen. A typical reaction to the showing of *LDV* at the Royal Academy's exhibition in 1941 appeared in the *Dundee Evening Telegraph*:

> One of the most striking pictures in the exhibition comes from Montrose. Mr. Edward Baird's study of a Local Defence Volunteer watcher on the hills has a powerful appeal. It suggests the strength of determination of Scotland and the part she is playing in the national effort. The tweed clad ghillie - who has imparted his martial spirit even to his dog - is typical of the resolve to defeat any attempt to invade the sombre fastness of Scotland portrayed in the picture.[7]

This and other reactions in the media show how easily the image was incorporated into Britain's wartime 'Culture of Defence'. With London under constant threat, the Royal Academy show was one way of claiming 'business as usual' in the nation's cultural diary. *LDV* was exhibited in a gallery themed as 'War Subject by Lesser-Known Artists'. The response of the *Dundee Evening Telegraph* shows the ease with which the painting was interpreted in terms of stereotypical Scottish identities: 'tweed clad', 'martial spirit' and 'sombre fastness'. This was certainly the opinion of the Ministry of Information, which bought the rights to reproduce the painting.[8] The image was used as propaganda in the Middle East, presumably as an illustration to colonial subjects of the determination of the 'mother country' to see the conflict through to the end. The themes that had animated the painting when it was known as *The Gamekeeper* were entirely lost in the more urgent discourse of the struggle between cultured freedom and culture-less tyranny.

At face value the image illustrated the determination of individual Scots to resist the threat of Nazi Germany as part of a broader British war effort. *LDV* was certainly used by the Ministry of Information in this context. Yet for Baird the figure in *LDV* was emblematic of a particularly Scottish identity, one very resistant to the standardising yoke of English/Britishness. These are themes that underpin Baird's wartime efforts in both formal oil portraits and pastel studies. His wartime art is double coded. Whilst contributing to the visual British war effort, Baird at the same time dissents from it in promoting a discrete kind of communitarian Scottish identity.

In 1940 the realities of this struggle would have been brought home decisively to Baird. With the German occupation of Norway completed by early June 1940, Montrose found itself within range of the Heinkel bombers of Hermann Goering's Luftflotte 5, based at Stavanger in the newly-conquered country. Between late 1940 and 1944 Montrose was the subject of frequent morale-sapping nuisance raids by small bomber formations. Dramatically, the town's broad High Street was strafed and bombed by three low-flying Heinkels in October 1940. Wartime restrictions meant that this event was not properly reported in the local media until early 1942:

> The last of the 1940 raids and the only one in which more than a single bomber took part was in the early evening of 25th October, when three planes in formation made a double run over the town and dropped about forty bombs…bombs fell in the river and one demolished a corner of the premises of Messrs. Chivers and Sons. Machine gunning all the time, the raiders dropped several other bombs at the North End of the town, went to St. Cyrus and machine gunned there, then circled the basin and came over Montrose again…It was probably one of the most exciting nights in the history of Montrose.[9]

Further raids caused material damage to the town Baird knew so well and resulted in civilian deaths. A nurse was killed when bombs fell on Sunnyside Royal Infirmary. A botched raid aiming to destroy Montrose's road and railway bridges killed three civilians and sank the coal boat, *The Duthie*, in Montrose harbour, a boat that Baird would have known well from the times he spent there. In this latter raid 'Pumphy' Davidson was elevated to the status of local hero by loosing off both barrels of his shotgun at the lone bomber - without result.[10]

During the dramatic historical events of 1940 Baird's daily routine continued comparatively unchanged. He made his way every morning from his mother's flat to the studio at 39 Bridge Street to continue work on the canvas in preparation. In the year of the country's greatest danger from German invasion, many British artists used what time they had to look back over their inter-war work and develop upon it in radically altered circumstances. In his still-life work and his representation of Ann Fairweather, Baird involved himself in this process of consolidation and re-evaluation.

1940 saw Baird embark on an unprecedented series of still-life paintings. He may have chosen to spend more time in the studio owing to new restrictions on civilian movement. Whatever the motivation, Baird stepped up his pace of work during the war. Nearly one third of his finished career output - twenty-five works in all - were completed in the war years. *Still-life with Flowers in a Glasgow Jug* (59) is a representative example of the four still-lifes completed by the artist in 1940. This particular painting was in part completed at the artist's home in the High Street in mid-1940 in response to a bowl of fruit that Baird's brother, David, by then enlisted in the Merchant Navy, had brought home from one of his voyages.[11] The sense of Baird's consolidation of his developed vision is all too apparent when one compares this painting with *Blue Cornflowers in a Dryleys Jug* from 1923. The composition of the tulips in the jug is very similar, although Baird's confidence in his abilities had increased sufficiently to incorporate the blue-leaf pattern of the jug into the work and the acutely-observed fall of light from a window on to the shining glaze of the vessel. The table top is tipped forward slightly towards the bottom left-hand corner of the painting, giving us a better impression of the volumes of the fruit and the striped pattern of the curtain draped over the table. For all the technical facility of the image, there is a distinct aura of unease in this work. The jug's pattern jars awkwardly with the multicoloured stripes of the curtain. The shiny glaze does not relate to the minutely-rendered skins of the apples to the left. Space in this composition is restricted and claustrophobic. These factors may well reflect Baird's broader social anxieties at the time.

Baird was also in an experimental mood in 1940. Another still-life, *Flower Piece* (61), shows him experimenting with a much thicker, bravura paint texture and freer draughtsmanship in representing a bunch of flowers in a vase. At about the same time he drew a monumental-scale nude of Ann reclining next to a bowl of apples and pears. Although this work is not dated, the rough nature of the paper, the drawing's execution in pencil only and the inclusion of the bowl of fruit all point to its completion contemporaneously with *Still-life with Flowers in a Glasgow Jug*. This reclining study clearly looks to the Mediterranean classicism of Matisse for inspiration and, through Matisse, further back to the French neo-classical portraitist, Ingres. Again this provides evidence of Baird revisiting important influences from earlier in his career. The image is a beautiful testimony to the closeness of his relationship with Ann and also fulfils a poignant commemorative function. It is possible that Baird completed this picture in case either of them were hurt or separated from the other in the event of invasion, perhaps with the intention to complete a finished portrait later. Sadly such a work was never executed.

Although his studio work had taken an introspective turn, Baird maintained his public profile by exhibiting *Monros* at the Royal Academy's annual exhibition in 1940. This exhibition was another symbol of cultural resistance to a foreign threat. *Monros* was displayed alongside work by Lowry, Paul Nash, Muirhead Bone and James McIntosh Patrick, placing Baird, appropriately, amongst artists of varied 'academic' and 'modern' credentials. On this occasion the critics emphasised the historical aspects of the painting:

> It might be described as a composite picture, for it embodies the principal landmarks of the town in a very unorthodox manner. The old suspension bridge, the river and the steeple - three old features of the town - are all worked in but no attempt has been made to place them in their relative positions. Instead, the artist has given a picture of how old Montrosians would visualise their native town and an impressive work of art he has made of it.[12]

Again the anachronistic elements of *Monros* acquired a powerful documentary and commemorative significance in wartime.

69 HARLEQUIN *61* FLOWER PIECE

Perhaps inspired by the successful reception of *Monros*, Baird began work on another large-scale view of Montrose in the late summer of 1940. Initially this took the form of a large pencil study provisionally entitled *Salorch*, an old Gaelic name for Montrose (this study has since disappeared).[13] By the following year *Salorch* had evolved into the oil painting *Montrose from Ferryden* (63). During the evolution of this canvas Baird found himself elected to the artists' committee for the newly-founded branch of CEMA in Montrose. By May 1941 the branch had appointed an executive to oversee the installation of an exhibition of modern art at the Upper Memorial Halls in Baltic Street. Chaired by James Carson, a good friend of Baird, the committee also featured John Rothnie, a close associate of Baird from the Workers' Education Association, and William Lamb. In the run up to the exhibition James Carson made the function of the Montrose CEMA clear:

We are fighting for our very material existence, but in the long run we are fighting for much more than that. We know that should the Germans get the upper hand it will be the end of everything we know in the way of spiritual and artistic matters as we appreciate them here.[14]

The exhibition opened in July 1941 with a strong Scottish content. Baird showed *Monros* and *Montrose from Ferryden*. Alongside the Colourists, J.D.Fergusson and S.J.Peploe, were younger Scottish painters such as William Gillies, William MacTaggart and John Maxwell. James Cowie, by then head of Hospitalfield School in nearby Arbroath, contributed three canvases. Until now we knew that Baird was an admirer of Cowie's work and perhaps responded to it in some of his portraits, but his presence at this exhibition provides clear evidence that the artists actually met.

These Scottish images were placed in a broader British and European context by the presence of paintings by Wyndham Lewis, Maurice de Vlaminck and Raoul Dufy. The committee had had access to the collections of Aberdeen Art Gallery and of John W. Blyth in Kirkcaldy. The show was not only an act of cultural defiance in the face of possible invasion, but also the first serious display of contemporary European painting in Montrose. Such a representative exhibition was quite unprecedented for the town, which up until then had only seen displays by local and amateur artists. Baird gave two well-attended lectures on the selection of works, and reports of these talks were extensively documented in the local press.

Eric Newton, then the high-profile art critic of the *Manchester Guardian*, opened the exhibition. In his remarks he had some criticism for Baird. At around this time Baird read Newton's introductory survey of European modernism, *European Painting and Sculpture*. His copy of Newton's book survives. It is littered in the margins with deprecating remarks, rubbishing Newton's ponderous formalism and highly relativistic analysis of the development of modernism. At one point a clearly exasperated Baird has inscribed 'Newton and others will speak of the representational process as a disability'. For his part, Newton contrasted Baird's two canvases in a defence of modern painting at the opening night of the exhibition and had some sharp criticism for *Montrose from Ferryden*:

> The word 'modern' had received an almost objectionable flavour these days…a distinguished artist who was at the exhibition that day [Edward Baird] had proved that they could paint a picture which looked exactly like a photograph. Into another picture the artist had put all sorts of imaginative qualities and probably the artist himself would say that the imaginative one was better. Artists should not try to act as a super colour camera.[15]

In two subsequent lectures Baird provided a comprehensive rebuttal of this rather literal interpretation of *Montrose from Ferryden* and outlined his dissatisfaction with modernism.

63 MONTROSE FROM FERRYDEN

He argued that pre-war modernism was 'an attempt to escape from a life which is too dreadful to face'.[16] Criticising the high number of still-life paintings in the show, he suggested that:

> This type of painting is popular. A man can hang it in his house and so escape from the world. He could look at it without getting any unpleasant reminders of the war…Fundamentally, it should be the artist's purpose not to permit that escape.[17]

For Baird - as is evidenced by *Montrose from Ferryden* - art was a direct appeal to the intellect as well as having educational and political functions. The appeals of art to the senses and to pleasure were very much incidental and secondary functions. Baird saw *Montrose from Ferryden* as a critique of the dehumanising standardisation and separation of modern life and the consequent erosion of community life. The artist had the privileged position of being able to undermine such trends:

> The modern world was becoming increasingly divided up and specialised; and the only man who could record its real unity was the artist - the painter, the writer, the musician, etc. Only they could show the man at the south end of the town what it was like to be a man at the north end of the town.[18]

In this light *Montrose from Ferryden* can be read as a defence of communitarian values against the specialization and separation of the modern, a trend exacerbated in conditions of war. Such a defence tied in closely with Baird's highly moral view of the function and purpose of art.

The painting's documentary qualities would have been particularly legible to those residents of Ferryden who knew the view very well. It was executed from a vantage point opposite Brownlow Place in Ferryden. The man in the boat approaching the shore would have been immediately recognised as Andrew Coull or 'Ferryboat Andra', who plied the Esk between Montrose and Ferryden. The identities of the children playing at the water's edge were also known.[19] Interestingly, the picture has a commemorative function, as it has been suggested that the small boat with the funnel, shown in the middle distance tied up in Montrose harbour, was the coal boat *The Duthie* destroyed in the German air raid of 1940.

Alongside these local references, the painting simultaneously functions for those not familiar with the area as a legible narrative of everyday life and the trade on which the town was built. For both locals and casual visitors it stands as a passionate engagement with contemporary reality, setting it apart from escapist modernism. In his lecture on the painting Baird laid great stress on his research into the development of Montrose:

> …he took great pains to show, in a scientific way, how the town was built up. First he drew the town itself…The pier and the boats on the foreshore were introduced, to counteract the tendency of the picture to run off at the right hand corner. He wanted the eye to alternate between the foreground

and the distance, so he introduced the group of children in the foreground and gave one of them a pink dress, of exactly the same shade as one of the houses in the distance. Instinctively the eye went from one to the other and that was the whole purpose of the group of children. There was something super-sharp and super-ordered about the whole painting and this was intentional. He was trying to show the order which underlies the world.[20]

This last observation is very telling. By means of a tightly-controlled draughtsmanship and colour composition, Baird seeks to convey an impression of order and calm, linking a local scene to a much broader desire for peace and stability. The painting stands as a deliberate engagement with a highly-idealised scene from contemporary life, subtly political yet readily legible for an audience unfamiliar with the language of modern art. It is both defensive of the community around Montrose harbour that made their living from the sea and related trades and on the offensive against the forces of modernism and tyranny that threaten to overwhelm it.

Baird's involvement with CEMA gave him a platform to raise his profile and develop his counter-hegemonic view of modernism that had simply not existed in peacetime. This platform also allowed him to advance an art engaged with reality as a viable and credible alternative to modernism, recording the lives of ordinary people in the fraught circumstances of conflict. Baird's career was at its peak in 1941. The Montrose exhibition attracted over 1,500 visitors in a fortnight, a highly impressive attendance. Baird's lectures and the popularity of both his exhibits saw a campaign started in the local press to secure one of his paintings.[21] In time Montrose Burgh Council purchased *Montrose from Ferryden* for an undisclosed sum. The huge success of *LDV* at the Royal Academy exhibition the same year saw it reproduced on the cover of *The Listener*, the widely-read BBC journal, in addition to reproduction rights being purchased by the Ministry of Information.[22]

Encouraged by all this success, in the second half of 1941 Baird began work on perhaps his best-known image, *Unidentified Aircraft* (68). The model for the tripartite figure pushed up against the picture plane in the foreground was Peter Machir. According to Machir's daughter, Baird felt that his friend had beautiful hands and wanted to include them in a painting. Until recently it has been assumed that the three heads in the painting represented a small crowd of people. We now know that the heads represent an unusually intense portrait of Machir seen from different viewpoints.[23]

Unidentified Aircraft stands as a complete statement of Baird's vision of art and also the role he saw art as fulfilling in wartime. As a basis for this statement he finally resolves any internal tensions in his representation of Montrose from the hill near Craig School. Of course this is now familiar as his mental image of the town, to which he had returned often from the late 1920s onwards. Here we are separated from the town by the wide expanse of the River Esk and by the three heads pushed up against the picture plane in the foreground. In his initial conception of the painting Baird had included searchlights positioned on the hills behind Montrose and a bomber. However these details were painted out when a visitor to the studio observed that the aeroplane would hardly be 'unidentified' if caught in searchlights. The angular and unusual townscape of Montrose is isolated on its peninsula and in the steely light of a 'bomber's moon' appears fragile and vulnerable. The limply-hanging cloud, transplanted almost directly from *Monros*, underpins this dramatic moment of desperate, fearful tension.

In the picture Peter Machir signifies the population of Montrose. The repeated heads give a sense of anxious movement, straining upwards toward the sky to try and pinpoint the aircraft. The upturned palm lends the piece a quasi-religious air of supplication. With the central actor, namely the aircraft, absent from the painting, our focus shifts to Machir as a dramatic emblem of the dangers and worry faced by the civilian population in wartime. The painting also reads as a record for Baird of the important landmarks of the town in case of extensive bomb damage.

Whilst images such as *LDV* were very readily interpreted as expressions of familiar Scottish subjectivities within the broader British war effort, canvases such as *Unidentified Aircraft* acted to undermine such cosy assumptions. Here history, popular cultural memory and the use of an ordinary working man as a symbol of a community under threat all combine to provide significant dissent from the standardising cultural narratives of wartime Britain. Although *Unidentified Aircraft* superficially ties in with the difficulties faced by Britain on the home front, the triple portrait of Machir and the painstaking composite view of Montrose lend the painting a uniquely Scottish aspect. Yet this painting was no parochial, reactionary intervention. By linking contemporary Scottish art with mainstream European art history and practice, Baird's wartime art looked forward optimistically to the time when Scotland could re-engage with a liberated Europe on cultural, rather than military terms.

Subsequent critical responses to the painting have named contemporaries such as James Cowie, the Flemish miniaturists and the Italian 'primitives' as important forerunners of the work. Although these are important to some extent, the real impetus behind this work lies in the coincidence of Baird's passionate identification with the town and community of Montrose and the threat that the passage of the war posed to that. Consequently the documentary and imaginative elements identified by Eric Newton in 1941 complement one another perfectly.

Unidentified Aircraft was submitted by Baird to a group exhibition entitled 'Six Scottish Artists', organised by Reid and Lefevre in its London gallery in May 1942. It has not been possible

68 UNIDENTIFIED AIRCRAFT

to establish who was responsible for organising the exhibition or the motivations behind it. Baird also contributed *Monros* and the pre-war portrait *Dan Crosse* (53), finished in 1938, which hung alongside works by Robert Colquhoun, Robert MacBryde, William Gillies, John Maxwell and William Johnstone. The catalogue of this show suggests an interesting compromise between the legacy of the inter-war Scottish Renaissance in the work of Baird and Johnstone and the 'Edinburgh School' as represented by Maxwell and Gillies. The exhibition also looked to future developments in facilitating the first major showing of Colquhoun and MacBryde's art. Both Ayrshire painters were embarking on careers that would see them make a decisive contribution to the development of European modernism in post-war London. For his part Baird was finally established in a position at the forefront of contemporary Scottish painting with a growing reputation as a painter who spanned both traditional and modern idioms.

The exhibition at Reid and Lefevre was well received. Writing in *Horizon*, the critic John Tonge asserted that:

> Edward Baird, who with his tighter handling and austere palette recalls Mantegna rather than the Frenchman working a *premier coup*, takes - and holds - his place amongst them…Baird is a sympathetic and penetrating portraitist, and paints the coasts and moors of Angus with a subtle stylisation…He is an interesting bridge between the traditional draughtsmanship of Bone and the modern movement.[24]

The exhibition was a success in financial as well as critical terms. Glasgow Corporation purchased *Unidentified Aircraft* for its Kelvingrove collection and Aberdeen Art Gallery bought *Monros*. Such purchases would not only have provided the artist with some much needed funds, but also the welcome feeling that his work would be seen in the context of contemporary European painting by much wider audiences than had been the case before the war.

The sales would also have helped Baird purchase new materials. By the spring of 1942, shortly after the completion of *Unidentified Aircraft*, he had found himself short of oil paint and lacking the funds to replenish his diminished stocks. At around this time Baird executed a detailed pencil portrait of Ann Fairweather, entitled simply *Ann* (67). This is a remarkable portrait as the artist has refused to let himself be hampered by his lack of materials. The determination in Ann's features, and the way in which he has captured the light in her eyes by the subtle gradations of tone and marking, show a continuing engagement with the 'representational function'. Simultaneously, the strange inverted lettering of the name 'INGRES' in the top right-hand corner bears witness to his continual re-evaluation of the neo-classical tradition.

A friend of Baird, local town planner and amateur author, John Angus, learned of his difficulty in acquiring materials and was able to offer the large collection of pastels and crayons belonging to his grandmother, who had recently died. Baird was delighted and began to complete portraits in pastel. His first completed work, *John Angus* (64), was done in return for his friend's kindness. *John Angus* sets the tone for most of Baird's wartime pastels. The portrait is more informal than the full-scale oil paintings and captures his friend's appearance against a neutral backdrop. This was the first in a series of pastel portraits that led to Baird securing employment as an Official War Artist.

In August 1942 there was a second exhibition of war art at Montrose that had a much broader 'British' focus. Baird did not show work himself, as he had been preoccupied with the exhibition at Reid & Lefevre. However he was involved with the selection of work and again gave well-attended lectures during the show. The selected paintings reflected Baird's input in terms of their documentary style and war subjects. Amongst the works were John Piper's interior of the ruined Coventry Cathedral, Edward Bawden's impression of the North African battlefield at Mersa Matruh and John Nash's *Damaged Submarine in Drydock*. Baird was quick to see these as evidence of a move away from high modernism in art:

> ...previous to the war, when you went into an art gallery, you saw skill of the highest artistic value but seldom did you see work of any merit which admitted that we had unemployment or even that we lived in a machine civilisation. The present exhibition shows a sudden turn about, a sudden turn to something very old; for, when art was at its strongest, it was not ashamed to serve civilisation.[25]

Baird clearly relished the direction that contemporary painting was taking during the war. In its engagement with political and social conditions he may have seen a vindication of his pre-war thinking. Certainly after the completion of *Unidentified Aircraft* Baird's wartime art took on a decidedly documentary and commemorative function. In part this documentary quality was stimulated by his appointment as a war artist. We are not sure of the precise motivations for his decision to become involved in this way, but it seems to have been encouraged by John Tonge.

After the success of the Reid and Lefevre show and encouraged by Tonge - and by his acquaintance with Muirhead Bone, who sat on the War Artist's Advisory Committee - Baird sent four pastel drawings to the WAAC in late 1942. Another portrait of Davidson, entitled *Home Guard* (65), was purchased immediately, but the Committee was hesitant on the quality of the other submitted drawings. In a letter Bone rather casually informed Baird that he would be kept in mind for future work in the north-east of Scotland, but that in the opinion of the Committee the pastels other than *Home Guard* were 'somewhat dull and stiff'. Baird was scathing of the reasons behind the WAAC's selection of *Home Guard* for purchase. In a letter to Tonge he suggested that:

> …it happened to fit in with the romantic dependable rustic role for which the English have cast the Scottish nation…for the subject not to fit this role is of course to be dull, and for the style not to be romantic is stiff.[26]

In spite of his disappointment at the Committee's reasoning, Baird nonetheless took advantage of what they could offer him. The first of these was a sketching pass, which admitted the artist to restricted areas and military bases. Baird applied for his pass in December 1942[27] and used it early the following year to complete a series of studies of Spitfire fighter aircraft and their pilots at RAF Montrose. These rough sketches feature typically exact reproductions of the famous lines of the Spitfire and an engagingly intimate sketch of pilots waiting in the dispersal area for take-off. It seems that Baird made at least one painting from the period. In his obituary of Baird Tonge mentions a painting showing Spitfires sweeping over the River Esk, but the image has long since disappeared.

At around this time Baird re-acquainted himself with his old Scottish Renaissance colleague, Fionn MacColla, who worked as a stores clerk at RAF Montrose for an unspecified period during the war. For a time the old friends seem to have fallen out, partly as a result of Baird's logical analysis of the failings of Scottish nationalism in the 1930s. An unsent letter to Dan Crosse reveals the basis of the dispute:

> …his intellectual stock in trade was only too glaringly the old fixations of his adolescent revolt, transmogrified here and there to suit the views of the Catholic religion…the man was a shocking mass of unresolved contradictions. At one point he was the young Catholic philosopher, intolerant of someone like J.B. Priestley, and the next he was relating with every appearance of approval some of the more delayed adolesencies of C.M. Grieve. One evening he would instruct us what fine fellows the English officers were once you had the privilege of meeting them, and the next he would be unable to concur with some Scottish nationalist opinion which did not assume that the English were complete fools on the grounds that it was not extreme enough for him.[28]

Baird's exasperation with MacColla reveals a more fundamental exasperation with the direction of political nationalism itself. From the anger in the tone of his letter it is clear that Baird still had a strong nationalist commitment, but was dismayed by the illogicality of the more fundamentalist wing of nationalism and, on a personal note, his impatience with his friend's intellectual inconsistencies. In his use of the word 'adolescent' Baird belies the seeming impossibility at that point of political nationalism ever making any gains in Scotland.

That Baird was still preoccupied with the potential of a re-awakened Scottish visual culture is evidenced in the extraordinary little imaginative sketch, *Harlequin* (69), dating from 1943. A Harlequin dancer, gaudily coloured, dances in front of a small orchestra to the right of the composition, with a backdrop of neo-classical architecture and a port scene. Clearly Baird is re-visiting his earlier career in this work. The architecture dates from his time in Italy and the orchestra is a direct echo of *Study for Sculpture* completed in the 1930s in collaboration with George Fairweather. St. Andrew's and Lion Rampant flags are clearly visible in the picture, making explicit that this was Baird's imagining of the potential of a Scottish art based on neo-classical values.

Baird was to be occupied with practical matters, however, as he entered the busiest period of his career. From March 1943 to April 1944 he completed three commissioned war portraits: *Mrs Barbara Garth* BEM (76), *Clydeside Munitions Worker* (70) and *K. Bennett* (71). He was paid ten guineas [£10.50] for each work. He spent some time in Glasgow, sketching these figures *in situ* at the Royal Ordinance factories at Bishopton and Cardonald to the west of the city.[29]

Whilst it is not difficult to see *Home Guard* as a stereotypical discourse of Scottishness, as happened in the critical response to *LDV*, it is more difficult to do so with other contemporary images such as *John Angus* or *Ann*. These portraits of friends and close family were personally significant as Machir-style emblems of the local community, but this did not translate to a wider audience. Baird's completed commissions for the WAAC used much the same documentary portrait technique. In works such as *Clydeside Munitions Worker* and *Mrs. Barbara Garth* BEM Baird continues to dissent from Britishness and a received view of the Scots by portraying them in a factual, unsentimental light. The methods he developed in portraying Montrosians as emblematic of their community extended in his commissioned war art to a broader reflection on the faces of contemporary Scotland.

During this period Baird continued to work on formal portraiture, completing *James Carson* MBE (74) during the latter part of 1943 as a commemorative portrait on Carson's retirement as superintendent of Rossie Farm School. Interestingly Baird employs a different technique of portraiture here. He completed a full-size painterly sketch of Carson before going on to produce the final portrait. His friend was surprised and delighted to receive the portrait as a gift from the school on his retirement and remembered fondly the interesting discussions he had had with the painter during his gruelling sittings at the Bridge Street studio.

Some portraits from this period are lost. It seems that Baird received through John Angus a commission to paint the daughter of the family living on the Balnamoon estate near Montrose. Known loosely as 'Miss Balnamoon', the painting was photographed at Bridge Street by local photographer Kenneth Hay during 1944-45. In one of the more well-known pictures of the artist himself, this work is shown on his easel in a completed state with a stooped Baird in his painter's smock next to it. However by this time Baird had taken so long in completing the portrait that the family no longer wanted it and its subsequent fate is unknown. Around this period Baird also completed a half-length portrait of Ann in a dark blouse, but there is no record of the whereabouts of this work either.

Baird's output tailed off abruptly during the second half of 1944. He seems to have suffered a severe attack of asthma and bronchitis and spent many months in hospital in both Montrose and Aberdeen. There were genuine fears for his survival to the extent that he married Ann whilst convalescing at home in early January 1945. As the war drew to a close Baird began to complete small-scale works again, such as his design for the jacket of MacColla's novel, *And the Cock Crew*, which was finally published that year. Although no one knew it at the time, with the end of the war Baird's career was also largely over.

Writing in *The Studio* in 1943 the gallery curator and critic, Tom Honeyman, observed 'There are many people in Scotland who are opposed to nationalism as a political philosophy, but many more who are completely in favour of nationalism as a cultural enterprise.'[30] In the war years Edward Baird typified such an attitude. Frustrated with the failure of political nationalism, he nonetheless continued to produce a series of portraits that negotiated between a discrete, local Scottish identity and the broader context of the defence of British and European culture in the battle against a philistine fascism. His art looked forward to a period when Scottish art could re-engage with European culture independently and on cultural rather than military terms. He took advantage of the growing profile of high culture in Montrose during the war and the development of a discrete local arts scene through the auspices of CEMA and the WEA. These bodies, as happened elsewhere in the UK, helped transform a rather *ad hoc* and dislocated pre-war art world into a unified group working hard for the first time to bring art to local people who had previously had little opportunity to see it. During the war provincial artists ceased to gravitate towards Edinburgh and London, but helped to build a patchwork of local scenes that assisted the establishment of a more democratic and inclusive post-war cultural polity.

6. 'I WILL BE DEAD MANY YEARS BEFORE SOMEONE RECOGNISES MY TALENT'

Farther north, Edward Baird of Montrose, and McIntosh Patrick of Dundee, have been working in almost Olympian isolation. There is nothing distinctively Scottish about Baird's work. He is a variously learned and platonic painter, whose beautifully designed compositions of curiously related material appeal more directly to the intellect than to the sense…in pursuing his laborious technique he may have a wary eye on the Flemish masters, but a style which is so closely related to the miniaturists seems today somewhat misplaced in point of time and provenance.[1]

So wrote T. Elder Dickson in the occasional journal *Scottish Art and Letters* in 1945. His comments are fascinating, as they clearly show the contemporary reception of Baird's work as somewhat puzzled and hesitant. Dickson clearly acknowledges the European context of Baird's painting, but he fails completely to respond to the discrete Scottish identities in his wartime art and overlooks the artist's idealistic attempts to try and establish a neo-classical element in Scottish visual culture.

Tragically Baird never fully recovered from his severe illness in the second part of 1944. In the four years that remained to him, he completed only one large-scale canvas. Many ideas for large-scale figurative paintings were developed, but none saw completion. Typical of these projects was the work called *Chapman off Angmagssilik* (79). The title derives from the British expedition to Greenland in the early 1930s led by the explorer and adventurer, Gino Watkins, who was killed during the trip. The expedition attracted much coverage during the period and led to a fast-selling book detailing the exploits of the party. One chapter deals with the art of sea-kayaking with descriptions of the British team demonstrating the kayak to local people. The chapter is well illustrated with black and white photos of the kayak and Baird seems to have composed his painting on the basis of these photographs.[2] As a picture it dealt with some familiar themes, such as man making a living from the sea, and is a powerful study of personal daring and exploration.

The artist seems to have been desperate to leave a large-scale figurative composition behind him. Aware that he was slowly dying, he worked intermittently over the three years from 1945 to 1948 on *The Howff* (78), which is a familiar cemetery in Dundee that Baird probably knew well from his visits to the city with Ann. The painting's incomplete, fragmentary nature is mute testament to the stifling of Baird's vision by his ill-health. A lonely Ann sits on a grave at centre right; in the background groups of figures, probably all Montrosians, talk quietly with one another. It is possible that the two elderly ladies standing to Ann's left are Baird's mother and Aunt Wilhelmina. Certainly *The Howff* reads as Baird's meditation on his impending death and the effect that that would have on those closest to him.

The one completed canvas from this period is *Angus and Mearns* (82), which was finished by mid-1948. It was commissioned by local farmer and future Labour MP, John Mackie, as a present for his wife's birthday. Baird would have begun work on it in late 1947 and, true to form, caused the purchaser much worry by taking so long to finish the painting. *Angus and Mearns* is an idealised composite landscape of the countryside surrounding Montrose. The work is not a realistic depiction, but an amalgamation of the memories that Baird had of the land he cared for so much. The picture is a study of rolling hills and meadows on a summer's day with the pale green of the fields bathed in a soft yellow light. In the right middle ground the spire of the Auld Kirk of Montrose, surrounded by a jumble of houses, rises from the fields of the Howe of the Mearns in a manner reminiscent of El Greco's studies of Toledo. The calm harmony of the countryside and town are thrown into confusion by Baird's last minute addition of the form of a red tractor, pushed up against the picture plane. In this sense Baird's composition re-visits earlier paintings such as *Birth of Venus* and *Unidentified Aircraft*. This added a discordant, jarring spatial note to the painting and encourages the viewer to consider the internal relationships of the composition more closely. Interestingly the fields are empty of farm workers and the land depopulated. Perhaps this was a final comment on the huge changes in the patterns of work and the relationships between town and country that Baird had witnessed during his lifetime.

Edward MacEwan Baird died in Montrose Royal Infirmary at 6.15 on the morning of 5th January 1949, just three weeks after his 45th birthday. His death certificate, signed by Ann, lists heart failure, chronic bronchitis and asthma as the causes. Tributes to Baird were immediate and heartfelt. An anonymous comment, probably penned by Ann, appeared in the *Montrose Review*:

> With the death of Edward Baird, Scotland has lost an artist of merit and an outstanding personality. It is as a painter that he would have preferred to be judged and remembered but in his native town of Montrose, where he lived and worked, we were better qualified to appreciate the man than assess the artist. Though illness had levied a terrible toll on his output, so that his achievements cannot be fairly measured against his forty-four years, it did not quench the vigour and keenness of his intellect and the courage and cheerfulness of his spirit….He truly loved his native town and people without expecting them to conform to his high ideals of which his criticism was an expression. As soon would he have expected his life to follow the pattern of his own desires. He had his consolations, a devoted household, friends, and was content. We have our memories and must be content also.[3]

Baird was cremated and his ashes scattered at Kinnaber, a favourite beauty spot of Ann and him just behind the far end of Montrose beach. We can only imagine Ann's feelings at the loss of her partner of over twenty years. Some time later she confided in a letter to Peter Machir's widow that 'I thought I would never get over it.'[4] The contents of his Bridge Street studio were packed up and returned to his rooms at 121c High Street, where, after the end of the period of mourning, plans took shape for a memorial exhibition in Dundee in June 1950. Ann and Baird's mother were involved in the exhibition, aided in choosing a venue and organising transportation of the works by many of his old friends, including James McIntosh Patrick, Allan Ogilvie, John Tonge and William Lamb. Indeed it was while he was hanging one of Baird's pictures at the Victoria Galleries in Dundee that Lamb fell from a ladder and badly damaged internal organs, leading to his untimely death in 1951.[5]

The memorial exhibition was a very representative selection of Baird's work and was well received. The catalogue was partly funded by the Scottish Arts Council and featured black and white illustrations of the major paintings, plus as complete a catalogue of the works as was

82 ANGUS AND MEARNS

possible. The opening of the exhibition in early June 1950 was extensively covered in the Scottish press. The *Montrose Standard* noted that 'it was a little puzzling that an artist of his kind should live in our midst and go unrecognised'.[6] Meanwhile John Tonge wrote a generous memoir of his old friend in the *Daily Record*:

> Quality he preferred to quantity. He saw the chief problem of the modern world, in fact, as the problem of maintaining quality amidst the pressure of quantity, of asserting the primacy of spirit over matter. Hence he was a nationalist.

> He might have become the Fantin of our day, so well could he render the bloom on a peach, the dewy shadow on an apple. Easily, with his impression of camel hair detail, he could have out-Dalied the Surrealist Dali, had he not been blessed with a robust distaste for the morbid and the lubricious. And in other circumstances he might have been a much sought after portrait painter…He painted best the people he knew, and best of all when he envisaged them about their work…[7]

Tonge's words now have a prophetic air, as the aspects of Baird's life he focused on are the ones that have been noted since, in particular his nationalism, his use of some Surrealist techniques in the works of the 1930s, his painstakingly literal representation and the firm moral purpose which he saw art as possessing. It is telling that Tonge's concluding remarks stress themes that run throughout Baird's art from his days as an undergraduate, namely, the interest in working people and the patterns of community that developed around that work.

All works not already in private collections were offered for sale at the memorial exhibition, but it seems that there were few purchasers.[8] In the years after his death Ann Baird seems to have had a lean time financially. Baird's mother died in early 1954. Sometime after that Ann left 121c High Street behind. She was much valued locally as a seamstress and also nursed for a period. In later life she was a well-known and liked Baillie on Montrose Town Council, still remembered for her character and dry humour. She died in 1972 and her ashes were scattered at Kinnaber as had her husband's twenty-three years before. At her death the bulk of Baird's paintings remained in her small flat.

By the time of Ann's death, Baird's reputation had picked up somewhat due to an exhibition of his paintings in Montrose in 1968 organised by Dr James Morrison. In the intervening years his work, represented in only a few public collections in Scotland, had been largely forgotten as his circle of friends slowly passed away, one after the other. The exhibition did much to re-establish Baird as an important figure in Scottish art in the 1930s and '40s, as did a further Montrose exhibition in 1981.

By the start of the 1980s art historians were beginning to look again at Scottish art, addressing themselves to questions of narrative, style and influence. With the commercial popularity of

Scottish art rising sharply from this time onwards, major historical surveys appeared written by Duncan Macmillan, Keith Hartley and William Hardie. Baird is mentioned in all these studies, but his atypical visual idiom, and the comparative lack of information about the development of his career, sees him occupy a peripheral place in accounts of Scottish painting.

In the research for this book Baird has emerged as an artist of high moral purpose, an individual passionately committed to his community and the people who lived in it. His determination to suggest a neo-classical Scottish art, rooted in the people he knew well and accessible to as wide an audience as possible, certainly sets him apart as an idiosyncratic figure in a visual culture that sought to build on the achievements of portraitists such as Ramsay and Raeburn by engaging with both Francophile colourism and Northern European expressionism. Baird's disdain for the more vapid explanations of modernism, his hard working perfectionism and his lifelong engagement with early Italian painting are evidenced in each one of his sensitive portrait studies and his imaginative responses to Montrose and its surroundings.

It may be difficult to fit such an unusual vision into broader narratives of visual culture in twentieth-century Scotland. However the breadth and quality of Edward Baird's output, bearing witness to a talent little recognised for too long, suggests that in the centenary year of his birth the task of reconnecting his vision with broader historical, aesthetic, social and political contexts has never been more urgent or necessary.

APPENDIX

EDWARD BAIRD: A PERSONAL MEMOIR

This is the text of a lecture delivered by the painter, James McIntosh Patrick, RSA, ROI, ARE, LLD (1907-1998), during the Baird exhibition at Montrose Museum in March 1981. The author gratefully acknowledges the kind permission granted by the Montrose Society to reproduce this important memoir here.

My friendship with Edward Baird began at the very start of our course in the Glasgow School of Art, when it so happened that not only were we the only two students to be allowed to go straight into the second year, but we found ourselves, by coincidence, in the same lodgings. We remained there together for almost six months before moving to another lodging, where we were joined by other art students, e.g. Sydney Shepherd (who, I think, later became head of one of the London art schools) and Vic Cormack. Other student friends used to come round in the evenings.

Baird was a pale, serious, rather delicate-looking boy with characteristic high shoulders. He had chest trouble aggravated by asthma and found the Glasgow weather more bearable than that of Montrose.

At first I was not sure what to call him but eventually I settled for 'Herr Baird' (I had done Higher German at school) and apart from a few people who called him 'Ted' most of us called him 'Herr Baird' for the rest of his time at college.

Baird had a subtle sense of humour and a rather oratorical style of speaking. On one occasion he gave a lecture on 'Hats' in Dundee College of Art couched in Biblical style, which was a resounding success.

We found we had a great deal in common. We joined the second year of the painting Diploma Course, so we missed lettering and some other General Course subjects. I do not think this would be allowed nowadays. The fact that we went straight into second year caused some resentment at first amongst the other students; we found it difficult to obtain space for our easels, for example. But the resentment eventually wore off and Baird became very popular.

In my view, Baird was a genius, unfortunately dogged by ill health. Indeed, he had so much ability that he could have turned his hand to almost anything. He had a very enquiring mind and so was too easily distracted, which could be troublesome for a painter. For instance, if he were painting a shotgun in a picture, he would want to know all about shotguns; he would go to the Library for information on them and soon would become an expert on their calibration, their range, etc. Again, if he were painting an eye, the work would stop for two or three weeks while he studied optics. In our second boarding house, the landlady's son, George, was an enthusiast on cars and would bother us about such technicalities as torque convertors and so on. Baird read up these matters and delighted in confounding George whenever he started talking about cars.

By the time we had started our second year, Baird was pursuing his own ideas. While the rest of us were progressing to bigger and bigger works, Baird was moving in the opposite direction, using smaller and smaller canvases. He worked much more slowly, too, so that, in the time it took us to paint a huge figure, Baird would paint only a foot or a hand. A fellow student called Anderson tended to draw in the style of Frank Brangwyn and worked very quickly indeed. On one occasion, when Baird had been drawing a head, Anderson came over to him and said 'Look, all you've done at the end of a week is to draw a nose, an eye and an ear - not even the back of the head or the hair on it'. Baird said nothing. He simply got up, walked across to Anderson's rather awful drawing, looked down and said 'Thy head is bloody, but unbowed'. A Baird remark like this was quoted in college over and over again.

We went to the life class every afternoon from four to six. Nobody ever missed it. Baird would sharpen an HB or a B pencil until the lead was about three quarters of an inch long and then he would use sandpaper on it until the point was like a needle. With this he could spend a whole week drawing only a hand. It may sound far-fetched to compare Baird with Leonard da Vinci, but there are similarities in their work. Baird would spend hours on a drawing, really searching out, just as Leonardo did. There is no doubt that, if he had had robust health, and if his painting career had not been cut short in 1949, this slow way of working would not have mattered because he would have had enough time. But, as it happened, his output was relatively small.

The man whom everyone in college revered was Maurice Greiffenhagen, whose highly-decorative work inspired many imitators. The nude shown in the Baird exhibition was done in Greiffenhagen's class but the technique is the antithesis of Greiffenhagen's.

Baird had a very strong individuality. He went his own way, no matter what other people were doing. There was probably no other student in Glasgow who was painting as he was. I was probably closest to him, as each of us influenced the other. We both believed, with the conviction of youth, that what was wrong with Scottish painting was that there had never been a classical school; practically all Scottish painting was romantic. We thought a lot of James Cowie, who was rather older than we were. We enjoyed his paintings.

Most Scottish painting, too, was very emotional, with plenty of brush marks. Fifty years ago the average Scottish painter thought he had improved on Cézanne if he could paint an apple with five strokes of a large brush whereas Cézanne had taken fifty strokes with a smaller brush. I also admired people like Stuart Park and Peploe. If one compares Cézanne and Peploe…one realises that Cézanne never gives the impression that it makes any difference whether it takes a week or a couple of hours to finish a painting. In Scottish painting the actual brush marks had to show and it had to be obvious where the artist flicked his wrist or used a palette knife. This style can have great charm and can generate a lot of excitement in the picture, but it has nothing to do with classical art. Hornel would often make pictures of snowdrops and little girls and the snowdrops would be done with a palette knife. If Baird painted snowdrops, they would have a careful botanical quality, which Baird considered important. The charm of much Scottish painting comes from the artist's thought and his brush strokes.

Of the portraits in the Baird exhibition, the head of Baird's uncle, the headmaster of Craig School, is in my view the finest head produced in Scotland this century. It is very like the man and has something of the quality of a Leonardo work.

As young painters, some of us were interested in an early Flemish technique of using a monochrome underbase glazed on top. If a white ground was used, the paint turned yellow with age, so that it darkened in tone. As the paint yellowed, however, it became more transparent, so that the darkening of the ground was compensated for. In Baird's painting, *W. Graham*, one can see how he reworked the squares of the chessboard and the chess pieces because the overpainted white ground has faded. The Knight has almost completely disappeared. This painting illustrates how difficult Baird found it to be satisfied with his work and how he kept reworking it. This painting also shows what a wonderful technique he had; the hands, the subtlety of the linen collar and the lenses of the spectacles reveal great technical skill.

The painting *LDV* was originally of a poacher but, when the war broke out, Baird added the armband. This is another superb painting. It appeared on the cover of 'The Listener'.

A second reworked painting, untypically practical of Baird, is *Unidentified Aircraft*. He painted this during the war from two of his earlier works - the pencil study *Figures with Montrose in the Background* and the oil painting *Monros*, both of which are in the Baird exhibition. Baird produced the pencil sketch in his Diploma year in the College of Art. A factory had just opened in the town. The sketch shows two ploughmen in the foreground set apart from a group of townies from the factory. The two groups of figures have different expressions and they are dressed differently. As well as being a composition, therefore, the study tells a story. This was characteristic of Baird. Baird worked on this drawing with his three-quarter inch pencil point like a needle and he drew and he drew and he drew. Finally, after weeks of work, he took the drawing into College where it disappeared. We finally discovered it crumpled in a ball in the wastepaper basket. Baird was nearly in tears and washed his hands of it. However, I took it back to our lodgings and held it in the steam from a boiling kettle till the whole thing was completely soft. Then I laid it on a board and stretched it out flat to remove the creases, and dried it. Baird later did some more work on it.

He used this drawing and the little oil *Monros* for his diploma painting, but this was never finished. He had only two months in which to finish it, which was not nearly enough for Baird. It should still be somewhere in the Glasgow College of Art and ought to be exhibited. Later on, during the war, he produced another version with three faces in the foreground and called it *Unidentified Aircraft*.

Baird's *Birth of Venus* was a wedding present to my wife and me. It rather shocked me as he painted so few pictures yet he gave this one away. He was our best man and, being a rather sentimental person, he chose Venus, the goddess of love, as the subject of the painting. About this time he was very friendly with George Fairweather who had a boat; hence the appearance of part of a boat in the painting. He often tried to pass on a private message in his paintings. Baird was a keen Scottish nationalist. He also greatly admired Botticelli and Crivelli, the Renaissance painters. Hence the 'Scottish Venus' as he called it arose out of his associations with a wedding, his involvement with Scottish nationalism, his love for messing about in boats and his love of Botticelli. The sky was painted on a red ground, which kept coming through, so that we had to wait a long time for the painting while Baird reworked it. Windsor and Newton had just brought out a new colour, Marsh Violet, and Baird used it to glaze the flower in the foreground. Unfortunately for Baird, an English painter, Wadsworth, used this technique later on and became famous down south. When people saw the 'Scottish Venus' for the first time, they thought Baird had been influenced by Wadsworth. I was horrified that Baird should want to give away his 'Scottish Venus' because it was one of the most complete works he had done.

I lost touch with Baird during my five and a half years in the army. His father-in-law lived only a few hundred yards from us in Dundee and Baird and his wife, Ann Fairweather, used to visit him so that I renewed our friendship after the war. Many of the paintings in the Baird exhibition were done while I was in the army. Baird was a remarkable man. It is very sad that he died so young. If he had lived, he could have been one of Scotland's finest painters.

CATALOGUE RAISONNÉ

The catalogue contains all of Baird's extant work and includes paintings that have since been lost or are in untraced private collections. In addition to provenance, an exhibition history is provided for each painting and, where appropriate, book, newspaper and journal references for paintings illustrated during the artist's lifetime.

References to exhibitions of Baird's work are as follows:

RA   Royal Academy, London
RSA   Royal Scottish Academy, Edinburgh
St Andrews 1935   *Modern Scottish Art*, The Whyte Gallery, North Street, St. Andrews, August 1935
Montrose 1935   Exhibition of local artists, Upper Memorial Hall, Baltic Street, Montrose, September 1935
Montrose 1941   *Contemporary Art*, Upper Memorial Halls, Baltic Street, July 1941 (organised by the Committee for the Encouragement for Music and the Arts, Montrose, together with the Workers' Education Association
London 1942   *Six Scottish Artists: Baird, Colquohoun, MacBryde, Johnstone, Maxwell, Gillies*, Reid & Lefevre, London
Dundee 1950   *Edward Baird 1904-1949*, Victoria Galleries, Dundee, June 1950
Montrose 1968   *Baird & Lamb* (organised by the Scottish Arts Council)
Montrose 1981   *Edward Baird*, Montrose Public Library, 1981
Edinburgh 1992   *Edward Baird*, Scottish National Gallery of Modern Art, Edinburgh, February-May 1992

All measurements are in centimetres (height x width); where not stated, dimensions are not known

Works included in the London exhibition in 2004 are marked with an asterisk *

1-25 *
SCHOOL DRAWINGS   (illustrated pp.20, 91, 99)

26 *
BLUE CORNFLOWERS IN A DRYLEYS JUG
oil on wood, 49 x 39, 1923   (illustrated p.23)
Private collection
Provenance: collection of Kenneth Tod, 1950; Allan Ogilvie C.A. by 1968
Exhibited: Dundee 1950 (17) as 'Cornflowers', Montrose 1968 (14), Montrose 1981

27 *
FAWN   (illustrated p.91)
tempera on wood, c.1926
Private collection
Provenance: passed from the estate of Ann Baird to present owners c.1972

28 *
NUDE   (illustrated p.95)
oil on canvas, 90 x 53, c.1926-27

Private collection
Provenance: passed from the estate of Ann Baird to present owners c.1972
Exhibited: Dundee 1950 (3), Montrose 1968 (2), Edinburgh, 1992 (1)
This was one of Baird's diploma paintings at Glasgow School of Art and won the Newbery medal in 1927

29
HALF-LENGTH NUDE   (illustrated p.95)
oil on canvas laid on board, 45 x 32, c.1926-27
Private collection
Provenance: passed from the estate of Ann Baird to present owners c.1972
Exhibited: Edinburgh 1992 (2)

30 *
STATUETTE   (illustrated p.91)
oil on canvas laid on board, c.1926-27
Private collection

Provenance: passed from the estate of Ann Baird to present owners c. 1972
Exhibited: Dundee 1950 (2), Edinburgh 1992 (3)

31
FIGURE COMPOSITION WITH MONTROSE BEHIND
pencil on paper, 25 x 29, c.1926-27   (illustrated p.15)
Private collection
This is a study for *32* below. In his Memoir of the artist James McIntosh Patrick remembers that Baird crumpled up the drawing and threw it in the bin in tears at some perceived imperfection. McIntosh Patrick rescued the drawing and smoothed out the creases. Apparently Baird added to the work in later years.

32
FIGURE COMPOSITION WITH MONTROSE BEHIND
tempera on wood, 85 x 112, 1927
Private collection
Provenance: passed from the estate of Ann Baird to present owners c.1972
Exhibited: Edinburgh 1992
Illustrated: Glasgow School of Art prospectus 1927-28, p.19

33 *
ADAM AND EVE   (illustrated p.27)
tempera on plywood, 17 x 19, 1928
Private collection
Provenance: passed from the estate of Ann Baird to present owners c.1972
Exhibited: RSA 1938 (257), Dundee 1950 (10), Montrose1968 (9), Montrose 1981, Edinburgh 1992 (5)

34
PORTRAIT OF A MAN
oil on canvas, c.1924-28 (?)
Private collection
Provenance: Ann Baird 1949-72
Exhibited: Dundee 1950 (no. 1), Montrose 1968, 1981
It has been suggested that the painting may have been a student work and the sitter a professional model at Glasgow School of Art. The handling of the paint certainly points to Baird's earlier career.

35 *
ROOFTOPS FROM THE PINCIO, ROME: ITALIAN SCENE
pencil on paper, 11 x 8.6, 1928   (illustrated p.27)
Montrose Museum, Angus District Museums Service
Provenance: not known
Exhibited: Edinburgh 1992
Illustrated: www.scran.ac.uk
Baird was in Italy by 16 December 1928 and made straight for Rome on the first leg of his travelling scholarship. He stayed at a guest-house in the Ludovici quarter of the city and this is likely to have been a view from his room. The date suggests that this drawing was the first completed by the painter on arrival in Italy.

36 *
NO UNION   (illustrated p.103)
stencil design for National Party of Scotland
1.5 x 2.0, c.1929-32 (original untraced)
Private collection
Provenance: on letter from Fionn MacColla to Peter Machir, March 1935
Both Agnes Valentine (née Machir) and Rona Pinterich (née Machir) identify this logo as having been completed by Baird. This is confirmed by Tonge's review of the memorial show at Dundee in 1950, where he refers to Baird 'making nationalist propaganda'. This image was forgotten until it turned up during the research for this book. It provides evidence of Baird's political commitment to Scottish nationalism in the early 1930s, which had waned somewhat by the war years. It was not unusual at this time for individual members to design their own logos and posters for political parties, when identifying symbols and colours varied from locality to locality, unlike the centrally-controlled party images of today. A search of the early NPS files at the National Library of Scotland, Edinburgh, did not turn up a reproduction of this image. This rather re-inforces the idea that Baird's logo was used only by the Montrose branch of the party. It may have been completed for Douglas

Elmslie's by-election candidature for Montrose Burghs in April 1932. As Nationalist candidate Elmslie came bottom of the poll, but still scored 1996 votes, 11% of the total - a respectable performance for a party that was still in its infancy. Baird's close friend, Allan Ogilvie, was Elmslie's election agent, whilst Andrew Dalgetty was Honorary Secretary of Montrose SNP for many years.

37

ITALIAN SCENE WITH NUDE
black ink on paper, 1929
Private collection
Provenance: passed from the estate of Ann Baird to present owners c.1972

38

MONASTERY OF ST. FRANCIS OF ASSISI
ink on paper, 1929
Private collection
Provenance: passed from the estate of Ann Baird to present owners c.1972
Exhibited: Montrose 1968 (36 or 41), Montrose 1981

39

ASSISI GATEWAY   (illustrated p.93)
tempera on board, 1929
Private collection
Exhibited: Dundee 1950 (49)

40

PORTRAIT OF A YOUNG SCOTSMAN
oil on canvas, 1931-32
Private Collection USA (or lost)
Provenance: bought by James H. Whyte from the RSA exhibition, summer 1933 and taken to the USA in 1940
Exhibited: RA 1932 (680), RSA 1933 (265),
St. Andrews 1935

*41 **

MRS OGILVIE   (illustrated p.37)
oil on board, 42 x 38, 1932
Private collection
Provenance: commissioned by Allan Ogilvie CA and

remained in his collection until his death.
Exhibited: Dundee 1950 (7), Montrose 1968 (6), Montrose 1981
Illustrated: cover of Memorial Exhibition catalogue, 1950
Born in 1903 as Susan Rachel Fergusson and descending from a St.Kilda family, she married Allan Ogilvie (1892-1968), a local chartered accountant, in 1928. Ogilvie organised a talk in Montrose in 1932 on the fate of the island of St. Kilda, at which his father-in-law spoke. Baird was in the audience that night. The portrait may have been commissioned in the same year, although the exact timeline of events is now lost. Susan Ogilvie died in 1996.

*42 **

MODERN ART A LONG WAY AFTER POOR PABLO AND HENRI
pencil and ink on paper, c.1925-26   (illustrated p.103)
Private collection
Provenance: completed c.1925-6 as a witty entry in a child's autograph book

43

SKETCH FOR CHOIR BOY
medium unknown, c.1932-33
Private collection
Provenance: passed from the estate of Ann Baird to present owners c.1972

*44 **

CHOIR BOY (Iain Pirie)   (illustrated p.97)
oil on wood, 65 x 54, 1933
Private collection
Provenance: passed from the estate of Ann Baird to present owners c.1972
Exhibited: Dundee 1950 (6), Montrose 1968 (5), Montrose 1981, Edinburgh 1992 (8)

45

WILLIAM MCCAUSLAND STEWART
oil on canvas 59 x 45, 1933
Private collection (whereabouts unknown)
Provenance: commissioned by the sitter, 1933
Exhibited: possibly St. Andrews 1936, Dundee 1950 (4),

Montrose 1968 (3), Montrose 1981
Illustrated: *Daily Record* 12 June 1950
William McCausland Stewart was a neighbour of
Edwin and Willa Muir in St. Andrews in the 1930s. It is
likely that Baird was introduced to Stewart through
James H. Whyte or John Tonge. McCausland Stewart
was a lecturer in French literature, whose career began
at Trinity College, Dublin in the late 1920s. Following a
spell on the academic staff at St Andrews University, he
moved to the University of Bristol, where he was made
Professor of French literature, enjoying a very
distinguished career.

46

SKETCH FOR 'BIRTH OF VENUS'   (illustrated p.95)
gouache on paper, c.1933-34
Private collection
This sketch clearly relates to *Birth of Venus* (47 below).
It shows a nude Ann standing at the water's edge on
Montrose beach. She is shown here from a different
vantage point than in the final painting, giving
evidence of the careful thought that Baird put into
composing the picture.

47 *

BIRTH OF VENUS   (illustrated p.40)
oil on canvas, 51 x 69, 1934-5
Scottish National Gallery of Modern Art, Edinburgh
Provenance: collection of James McIntosh Patrick,
1935-98; accepted by H.M. Treasury in lieu of tax and
allocated to SNGMA, 2002
Exhibited: Montrose 1935, Dundee 1950 (5), Montrose
1968 (4), Montrose 1981, Edinburgh 1992 (10)
Illustrated: T.J. Honeyman, 'Art in Scotland', *The
Studio*, vol.CXXVI, no.606, September 1943, p.75
This painting was a wedding present from Baird to
James McIntosh Patrick. Baird was McIntosh Patrick's
best man at his marriage in 1934. Characteristically,
the work was not finished for some months after the
wedding and reverted to Baird until a brief public
exhibition in Montrose in September 1935.

Subsequently Baird had the painting in his studio for a
period during the war. Mrs. Agnes Valentine, model for
Girl Guide (66 below), remembers it in Baird's studio
at 39 Bridge Street during 1942.

48 *

GEORGE FAIRWEATHER FRIBA   (illustrated p.8)
oil on canvas, 60 x 51, 1935
Scottish National Portrait Gallery, Edinburgh
Provenance: George Fairweather, 1935-86; Private
Collection, 1986-92; SNPG since August 1992
Exhibited: RSA 1936 (264), Dundee 1950 (8), Montrose
1968 (7), Montrose 1981, Edinburgh 1992 (11)
Illustrated: 'The Art of Scotland', *The Studio*, vol.CXII,
no.520, July 1936

49 *

THE FIFIE   (illustrated p.93)
watercolour, 1936
Private collection
Provenance: George Fairweather, c.1936-1986; Private
Collection since 1986
Exhibited: Dundee 1950 (51) as 'Fishing Boat',
Montrose 1968 (38), Montrose 1981
The Fifie was a local fishing boat. In an undated letter
to George Fairweather, Baird commented at length on
the origins and development of this type of boat: '...My
excuse for making such a documentary drawing of the
fishing boat is that it is a type with a history which
with the wanton destruction of inshore fishing is likely
to come to a close.' The painting is unusual, as Baird
seems to have completed the work in a day at
Montrose harbour. Whilst this rapidity will have been
dictated in part by the nature of the medium, such
speed of completion was very unusual for the artist.

50 *

WALTER GRAHAM   (illustrated p.46)
oil and tempera on canvas, 92.1 x 71.7, c.1936-7
McManus Galleries, Dundee
Provenance: the Artist; Ann Baird 1949-1968;
purchased by Dundee City Council 1968

(TOP)
FOUR PAGES FROM A SKETCHBOOK FROM SCHOOLDAYS

(CENTRE)
27 FAWN

(BOTTOM left to right)
30 STATUETTE
STILL-LIFE COMPOSITION FROM SCHOOLDAYS

91

Exhibited: RSA1937 (99) as 'W W Graham Esq.',
Dundee 1950 (22), Montrose 1968 (19), Montrose
1981, Edinburgh 1992 (12)
It has been suggested that Walter Graham became
something of a father figure to Baird after the death of
the artist's father at sea in the late 1900s. A
schoolmaster, Graham married Baird's Aunt,
Wilhelmina Brechan. After the death of Baird's father,
Graham took a closer interest in his nephew and may have
played a role in encouraging him to study at art school.

51 *

DISTRESSED AREA   (illustrated p.53)
oil on wood, 38 x 50, c.1936-38
Private collection
Provenance: George Fairweather c.1938-86; family
collection to c.1994; private collection from c.1994
Exhibited: RSA 1938 (412), Dundee 1950 (11),
Montrose 1968 (10), Montrose 1981, Edinburgh 1992
The painting may have been named after George
Malcolm Thompson's book, *Scotland, that Distressed
Area* which appeared in 1935. Thompson was a political
and economic commentator who was sympathetic to
the emergent SNP in the 1930s, blaming much of
Scotland's structural weaknesses on remote rule from
Westminster. The painting shows the boating shed of
Alicky Brannan on Rossie Island, which has now been
obliterated by the works of the Montrose Oil Basin.
There have been suggestions that Baird occasionally
used the shed as a studio. George Fairweather and he
built it in an attempt to do something for the
unemployed of Montrose in the 1930s. Ambitious plans
for an artists'/workers' commune there failed to come to
fruition. During the war the hut became something of a
social venue for the Workers' Education Association and
for Christmas parties for local children.

52

PORTRAIT OF A MAN   (illustrated p.97)
oil on canvas, probably late 1930s
Private collection

Provenance: the artist; Ann Baird 1949-72
The style of this portrait probably dates it to the late
1930s. The subject is not definitely known, but
contemporary photographs suggest that it may be Tom
Whitson, a local solicitor with whom Baird was friendly.

53 *

DAN CROSSE   (illustrated p.97)
oil on wood, 32 x 16, 1938
Private collection
Provenance: the artist to 1949; Ann Baird 1949-72;
passed from estate of Ann Baird to the present owners
c.1972
Exhibited: London 1942 (5) Dundee 1950 (19),
Montrose 1968 (16), Montrose 1981, Edinburgh 1992 (14)
Dan Crosse was a school friend of Baird and Fionn
MacColla. He countersigned contractual documents
relating to MacColla's *The Albannach* in 1932 and was
active in the NPS in the thirties. Crosse went into the
forces during World War II, which he survived, but his
fate subsequent to that is unknown.

54 *

HIGH STREET, MONTROSE   (illustrated p.93)
watercolour, 1938
Private collection
Provenance: Provost J. Butchart from 1938;
subsequently private collection.
Exhibited: Montrose 1968 (35), Montrose 1981
The painting was executed from a vantage point about
100 yards south-west of the Old Kirk, near the
intersection of High Street and Bridge Street. It may
even have been completed at Baird's first studio at 3a
Bridge Street, which he occupied in the late thirties.

55 *

MONROS   (illustrated p.56)
oil on canvas, 36 x 51, 1939
Aberdeen Art Gallery and Museums
Provenance: bought from the artist 1942
Exhibitions: RSA 1939 (264), RA 1940 (428), Montrose
1941, London 1942, Dundee 1950 (9), Edinburgh 1992 (16)

(TOP left to right)
54 HIGH STREET, MONTROSE
39 ASSISI GATEWAY
49 THE FIFIE

(CENTRE)
79 CHAPMAN OFF ANGMAGSSILIK

(BOTTOM left to right)
81 MUSEUM PIECE
60 FLOWERS IN A GLASGOW VASE

Illustrated: as 'Montrose' in John Tonge, 'Scottish Paintings', *Horizon*, vol.V, no.29, May 1942, pp.331-35

56 *

LOCAL DEFENCE VOLUNTEER   (illustrated p.60)
oil on canvas, 91.5 x 71, 1937-9
Scottish Arts Council
Provenance: the artist; Ann Baird, 1949-50; bought by Scottish Arts Council in June 1950; currently on long term loan to Aberdeen Art Gallery
Exhibited: RA 1941(429), RSA 1942 (577), Dundee 1950 (21), Montrose 1968 (18), Montrose 1981, Edinburgh 1992 (15)
Illustrated: front cover of *The Listener*, vol.25, no.643, 8th May 1941
The painting was begun sometime in 1937 and was almost complete in September 1939 when war broke out. Originally entitled 'The Gamekeeper', Baird subsequently added the Local Defence Volunteer armband to the portrait and the piece assumed its present title. The subject of the painting, James 'Pumphy' Davidson, was a casual labourer, wildfowler and poacher. He had been a friend of Baird since meeting at Montrose Harbour in the 1920s. He was one of the first men in Montrose to volunteer for service with the LDV, which became the Home Guard in mid-1940. Davidson is also the subject of the later chalk and pastel sketch *Home Guard* (*65* below) dated 1942.

57

BLACK LABRADOR PUPPY
pastel & charcoal on paper, 1939
Private collection
Provenance: owned by Kenneth Tod in 1950 and passed around various collections; now in a private collection
Exhibited: Dundee1950 (48), Montrose 1981
This is the same dog as in *LDV* (*56* above). The puppy was too restless to sit still for Baird, so he completed this drawing and the painting of the dog in *LDV* from studio photographs, some of which are now in a private collection.

58

NEAR LUNAN
watercolour, 1939
Private collection
Provenance: formerly in the collection of Allan Ogilvie C.A.; it has since been acquired by a private collection
Exhibited: Dundee 1950 (50), Montrose 1968 (37), Montrose 1981

59 *

STILL-LIFE WITH FLOWERS IN A GLASGOW JUG
oil on canvas, 45.9 x 61, 1940   (illustrated p.6)
Scottish National Gallery of Modern Art, Edinburgh
Provenance: uncertain
Exhibited: Dundee 1950 (16 or 18), Montrose 1968, Montrose 1981, Edinburgh 1992 (17)

60

FLOWERS IN A GLASGOW VASE   (illustrated p.93)
1940
Angus District Museums Service
Provenance: unclear, but in the possession of Angus District Museums Service by 1981
Exhibited: Dundee 1950 (16 or 18), Montrose 1968 (13), Montrose 1981

61 *

FLOWER PIECE   (illustrated p.65)
oil on canvas, 59.7 x 49.5
Private collection
Provenance: Ann Baird to 1950; private collection
Exhibited: Dundee 1950

62

FLOWER PIECE
oil on board, 1940
Private collection

63 *

MONTROSE FROM FERRYDEN   (illustrated p.67)
oil on canvas, 43 x 60, 1941
Angus District Museums Service
Provenance: seemingly in the collection of Montrose Burgh from the early 1940s, although acquisition date is unclear

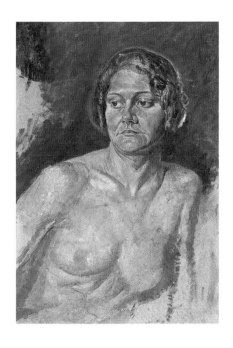

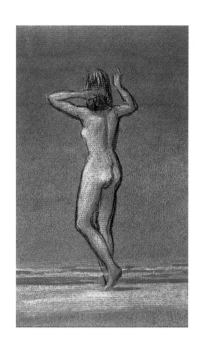

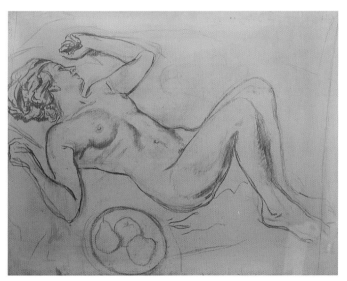

(TOP left to right)

29 HALF-LENGTH NUDE

28 NUDE

46 SKETCH FOR 'BIRTH OF VENUS'

(BOTTOM)

87 RECLINING NUDE

Exhibited: Montrose 1941 as 'Montrose Harbour', Dundee 1950 (12) as 'Montrose', Montrose 1968 (11), Montrose 1981, Edinburgh 1992 (19)
Illustrated: www.angus.gov.uk/artists/baird.html
This painting was a view of Montrose and the River Esk seen from opposite Brownlow Place in Ferryden. The man in the boat was a local ferryman, Andrew Coull, known as 'Ferryboat Andra'.

64 *

JOHN ANGUS   (illustrated p.97)
chalk and pastel on paper, 1942
Private collection
Provenance: private collection since 1942
Exhibited: Dundee 1950 (42), Montrose 1968 (30), Montrose 1981
John Angus was a town planner and short story writer, whose work occasionally appeared in *The Scotsman*. He knew Baird reasonably well. The portrait came about after Angus offered his late mother's chalk and pastels to the painter, who was running low on materials. Baird was delighted and offered to do a portrait in return.

65 *

HOME GUARD   (illustrated p.99)
chalk on paper, 1942
Aberdeen Art Gallery & Museums
Provenance: bought by War Artists Advisory Committee, November 1942; allocated to Aberdeen by 1948
Exhibited: Dundee 1950 (36), Montrose 1968 (27), Montrose 1981
At the suggestion of John Tonge Baird sent four drawings to the War Artists Advisory Committee in November 1942, offering them for sale and providing samples of his work. The Committee acquired this painting for seven guineas, but rejected the others (the sample probably included *64* above and *66* and *67* below). Subsequently Muirhead Bone, a member of the Committee, wrote to Baird criticising the unsold works as 'rather dull and stiff'. Nonetheless Baird acquired a sketching pass from the Committee in December 1942, which gave him much greater freedom to draw in restricted areas, including RAF Montrose. Three commissions followed from the WAAC in 1943, making Baird an Official War Artist.

66

GIRL GUIDE
pastel on paper, 1942
Private collection, Edinburgh
Provenance: formerly in the collection of Allan Ogilvie; private collection since c.1990
Exhibited: RSA 1943 (824) as 'Agnes Machir', Dundee 1950 (40), Montrose 1981
The subject is Peter Machir's eldest daughter, Agnes, who sat for the portrait aged 11. Baird later attempted to draw Agnes's younger sister, Rona, in his own version of Thomas Gainsborough's *The Blue Boy*. However the child was too small to submit to the exacting discipline required of Baird's subjects and the attempt was abandoned.

67 *

ANN   (illustrated p.99)
pencil, pastel & charcoal on paper, 1942
Private collection
Provenance: George Fairweather from the 1940s to 1986; private collection since 1986
Exhibited: Dundee 1950 (37), Montrose 1968 (42), Montrose 1981
This sketch seems to show a slightly older Ann. Interestingly, the word 'INGRES' is shown inverted in the top left-hand corner of the sketch, suggesting that Baird was paying homage to the work of the great French neo-classical painter.

68 *

UNIDENTIFIED AIRCRAFT   (illustrated p.71)
oil on canvas 71 x 91.5, 1942
Glasgow Museums and Art Galleries, Kelvingrove
Provenance: acquired by Glasgow Corporation c.1942-43

44 CHOIR BOY (IAIN PIRIE)

52 PORTRAIT OF A MAN

53 DAN CROSSE

64 JOHN ANGUS

Exhibited: London 1942, Dundee 1950 (23), Montrose 1968 (20), Montrose 1981, Edinburgh 1992 (20)
Illustrated: Glasgow Museums Journal, 1945-6, 'Wartime Acquisitions'
The painting features Baird's close friend and eventual best man, Peter Girvan Machir. Baird thought that his friend had beautiful hands and wanted to include them in a painting. It seems that the work initially featured searchlights raking the skyline and the outline of an aircraft, but these were later painted out by the artist when it was pointed out that the aircraft would not be 'unidentified' if caught in searchlights. As a result the skyscape and outline of Montrose are remarkably similar to the earlier painting *Monros* (55 above)

69 *

HARLEQUIN   (illustrated p.65)
oil on board, 1943
Private collection
Provenance: the Artist; Ann Baird 1949-72; passed from the estate of Anne Baird to a Montrose private collection c.1972

70 *

CLYDESIDE MUNITIONS WORKER
pastel on paper, 1943
Glasgow Museums and Art Galleries, Kelvingrove
Provenance: commissioned by the War Artists Advisory Committee 1943; WAAC, 1943-47; allocated to Glasgow Corporation by 1948
Exhibiteds: Dundee 1950 (44), Montrose 1968 (32), Montrose 1981
The subject is an unidentified worker for the Royal Ordinance Factory at Cardonald near Glasgow. Baird had been asked to sketch a Miss Catherine Munro, who worked at a Ministry of Supply factory in Powfoot, Dumfriesshire. However Miss Munro was given indefinite special leave in July 1943 at the time that Baird was due to sketch her and he was directed to Cardonald by way of replacement. Baird would have

completed this image during late summer and autumn 1943; it was sent to London on 27th November.

71

K. BENNETT
chalk on paper, 1943
McManus Galleries, Dundee.
Provenance: commissioned by the War Artists Advisory Committee, 1943; WAAC, 1943-48; presented to Dundee, August 1948
Exhibited: Dundee1950 (43), Montrose 1968 (31), Montrose 1981
Commissioned in March 1943 and completed by 16th August that year. Bennett was a worker at the Royal Ordinance Factory at Bishopton, Renfrewshire, although nothing more is known about him. Baird was paid ten guineas [£10.50] for the portrait. After the war the WAAC allocated it rather randomly to the McManus Galleries in Dundee in August 1948.

72

SOUTH ESK
oil on canvas, 51 x 61
Private collection
Provenance: formerly in collection of Lawrence Ogilvie
Exhibited: Dundee 1950 (20), Montrose 1968 (17), Montrose 1981

73

DAVID BAIRD
chalk on rough paper, 48 x 35, 1944
Private collection
Provenance: the Artist; David Baird from c.1949; acquired by present owners after David's death in the mid-1970s
Exhibited: Dundee 1950 (41), Montrose 1981
David Baird was Edward's younger brother, born in December 1909. In peacetime he ran confectioners and tobacco shops, but during the war he served on the dangerous Merchant Navy convoys from Scotland to Murmansk. He spoke fluent German and therefore his skills as a Signals Officer were highly prized. Sometime

65 HOME GUARD

67 ANN

PORTRAIT SKETCH AT ART SCHOOL

74 JAMES CARSON MBE

after the war, he moved to Liverpool, where he died in the 1970s. Baird offered this work for sale to the WAAC in late April 1944 under the title 'Signals Officer, Merchant Navy', but it was rejected.

74 *

JAMES CARSON MBE   (illustrated p.99)
oil on canvas, 89 x 69, 1944
Scottish National Gallery of Modern Art, Edinburgh
Provenance: Rossie Island School near Montrose until c.1968; Carson family, Derbyshire & Sussex to 1996; SNGMA since 1997
Exhibited: Dundee 1950 (15), Montrose 1968 (12), Edinburgh 1992 (23)
Carson was a very well-known figure in Montrose. Born in Dalry, Ayrshire, he was Superintendent at Rossie Island School near Montrose from 1897-1900 and then 1903-43, when he retired.
Carson had a very busy public life, being chair of Angus & Kincardine Library Committee, involved with the local scouts, and Chair of the Montrose branch of the Workers' Education Association. It was in this latter capacity that he is likely to have encountered Baird, as the two wartime exhibitions were organised in part by the WEA. The portrait was commissioned by Rossie Island School to mark Carson's retirement and hung there until his death at Brechin in August 1963.

75

JAMES CARSON MBE
oil sketch on canvas, 1943-44
Angus District Museums Service
Provenance: Carson family 1943-96; Angus District Museums Service since 1997

76 *

MRS BARBARA GARTH BEM   (illustrated p.101)
pastel on paper, 1943-44
Paisley Museum and Art Gallery
Provenance: commissioned by War Artists Advisory Committee 1943; WAAC 1944-47; allocated to Paisley by 1948

Exhibited: Dundee 1950 (45), Montrose 1968 (33), Montrose 1981
Barbara Garth was a Chargehand at the Royal Ordinance Factory in Bishopton. Little is known about her, other than that she was gazetted for her service and presented with the British Empire Medal by King George VI at Buckingham Palace on 6th June 1944. This was the last of Baird's WAAC commissions, which was completed and sent to London in April 1944.

77

DESIGN FOR COVER OF 'AND THE COCK CREW'
watercolour, c.1938-45.
Exhibited: Dundee 1950 (53) as 'Book Cover'
MacColla's novel was begun in 1934. The manuscript was ready for publication in 1938, but the outbreak of war meant that it did not appear until 1945. 'And the Cock Crew' is one of the most powerful and evocative works of fiction concerning the Highland Clearances, the clash of Gaeldom and Anglophone culture, and the crisis of conscience that afflicted many during that dreadful time. Baird contributed the striking dust jacket image of a cockerel, which appeared on the first edition. The long gestation of the project makes the actual date of the image a mystery.

78 *

THE HOWFF   (illustrated p.79)
oil on board, 122 x 202, c.1945-48 (unfinished)
Private collection
Provenance: the artist; Ann Baird 1949-72; private collection
Exhibited: Dundee 1950 (30), Edinburgh 1992 (33)

79 *

CHAPMAN OFF ANGMAGSSILIK   (illustrated p.93)
oil on canvas, 43 x 61, c.1945-48 (unfinished)
Private collection
Provenance: the artist; Ann Baird 1949-72; private collection
Exhibited: Dundee 1950 (26), Montrose 1968 (22), Montrose 1981

76 Mrs Barbara Garth bem

83 Portrait of a Man with Pipe

86 Princess Magnolia

96 Sketch of a Man

80

STUDY FOR 'CHAPMAN OFF ANGMAGSSILIK'
oil on canvas, c.1945-48
Private collection
Provenance: the artist; Ann Baird 1949-72; private collection

81

MUSEUM PIECE   (illustrated p.93)
oil on canvas, 50 x 90, c.1945-48 (unfinished)
Private collection
Provenance: collection of George Fairweather; acquired by private collection after 1986
Exhibited: Montrose 1981, Edinburgh 1992 (30)

82 *

ANGUS AND MEARNS   (illustrated p.80)
oil on canvas, 68.5 x 89, 1948
Private collection
Provenance: commissioned by John Mackie 1947-8; private collection since 1948
Exhibited: Dundee 1950 (24), Montrose 1968 (21), Montrose 1981, Edinburgh 1992 (32)
This is Baird's final finished oil painting. John Mackie commissioned it as a birthday present for his wife and was much exasperated by the length of time the artist took to complete the work. Mackie was very active in the Labour Party and was later an MP.

83

PORTRAIT OF A MAN WITH PIPE   (illustrated p.101)
pastel on paper, c.1942-45
Private collection
Provenance: the Artist; George Fairweather to 1986; private collection
Exhibited: Dundee 1950 (34) as 'Smiling Man', Montrose 1981

84

DESIGN FOR MURAL
pencil on paper
Private collection
This long mural shows a procession of figures and farmyard animals, perhaps figures for the monumental painting that Baird planned, but never achieved. The work is similar in nature to the cartoon of 'The Holy Family'(*85* below). It could be dated either to Baird's student days (1924-27), when he drew extensively in a very sharp pencil, or to the last few years of his life, when his ability to work consistently was hampered by deteriorating health.

85

THE HOLY FAMILY   (illustrated p.103)
pencil on paper
Private collection
Exhibited: Montrose 1968 (45 or 46)

86

PRINCESS MAGNOLIA   (illustrated p.101)
pencil on paper, c.1942-1944
Private collection
Provenance: collection George Fairweather from the 1940s-1986; private collection
Exhibited: Dundee 1950 (35), Montrose 1968 (26), Montrose 1981
The subject of this drawing remains obscure. Allegedly Baird looked out of the window of 121 High Street and saw a very attractive lady, whom he subsequently drew. However, given his slow working methods, it is unlikely that such a detailed work could have been constructed from a fleeting glimpse of a stranger.

87 *

RECLINING NUDE   (illustrated p.95)
pencil on paper, 1940s
Private collection
This is a large-scale portrait of the artist's wife next to a bowl of pears and apples. The quality of the paper and the intimate nature of the subject suggest that this may have been done towards the end of the war, possibly around the time of their wedding in January 1945.

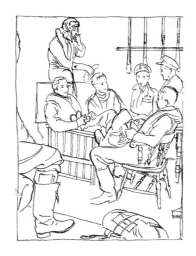

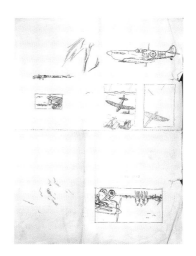

(TOP left to right)

36 NO UNION
85 THE HOLY FAMILY

(CENTRE)

42 MODERN <u>ART</u> A LONG WAY <u>AFTER</u> POOR PABLO AND HENRI

(BOTTOM left to right)

89 DESIGN FOR SCULPTURE
92 GROUNDED, MONTROSE AERODROME
93 SKETCHES OF SPITFIRES IN FLIGHT

88
NUDE
ink and wash on paper
Private collection
Provenance: Ann Baird to 1972, when it passed to the present owners
This is a very intimate sketch of the artist's wife that can be dated to any time from the early 1930s onward

89 *
DESIGN FOR SCULPTURE   (illustrated p.103)
red ink on paper, mid-1930s
Private collection
Provenance: George Fairweather to 1986; private collection

90
THREE SKETCHES FOR UNIDENTIFIED
AIRCRAFT/SOUTH ESK
ink on paper, c.1941-43
Private collection

91
THREE SKETCHES FOR CHAPMAN OF ANGMAGSSILIK
ink on paper, c.1944-48
Private collection

92 *
GROUNDED, MONTROSE AERODROME
ink on paper, c.1942-44   (illustrated p.103)
Private collection

93
SKETCHES OF SPITFIRES IN FLIGHT (illustrated p.103)
ink on paper, c.1942-44
Private collection

94
AIRCRAFT & BOATS
ink on paper, c.1942-44
Private collection

95
SUSPENSION BRIDGE, MONTROSE
pencil drawing

Private collection
Provenance: collection of Mrs Dalgety in 1950; subsequently private collection, Montrose
Exhibited: Dundee 1950 (33)

96
SKETCH OF A MAN   (illustrated p.101)
pencil and pastel on paper, probably c.1942-44
Private collection
The style and medium of this work probably date it to wartime, after Baird began using pastel in mid-1942. The subject is unknown.

LOST WORKS

97
PORTRAIT OF A WOMAN
c.1942-1944
Illustrated: www.angus.gov.uk/artists/baird.html
There are two photographs of this work, both taken by Kenneth Hay during a visit to 39 Bridge Street in either 1944 or 1945. One is a photograph of the painting itself and the other features the painting on an easel in the background of the best known photograph of Baird. It has been suggested that the painting is of Miss Balnamoon, daughter of a well-off local family, who commissioned the portrait from Baird at the suggestion of John Angus (*64* above). Presumably this would have been between 1942 and 1944. However Baird took so long to finish the painting that the family did not want it by the time it was ready. Its current whereabouts are unknown.

98
BETTY
pastel on paper, 28 x 38.1, 1942
Provenance: listed in the collection of Roy Fairweather, but not seen since 1968
Exhibited: Dundee 1950 (39), Montrose 1968 (28)

99

TERRIER AND BALL ON MONTROSE BEACH
oil on canvas, late 1930s
A photograph of this lost work is in a private collection.
There are no exhibition records of the painting or
references to it in secondary literature. Contemporary
photographs suggest that the dog, a Jack Russell terrier,
belonged to Walter Graham (*50* above)

100

ANN BAIRD
oil on canvas, c.1943
Exhibited: possibly RSA 1943 (849)
Only a small photograph of this painting exists, taken by
Kenneth Hay during a visit to Baird's studio in either 1944
or 1945. This may have been 'Ann' exhibited at the RSA in
1943. There are no references to it in secondary literature.

101

MRS FORD THOMSON
oil on canvas, possibly late-1930s or 1940s
Provenance: in the collection of Ford Thomson until
c.1981; present whereabouts unknown
Exhibited: Dundee 1950 (14), Montrose 1968,
Montrose 1981
The sitter was the wife of a local surgeon. Older
residents of Montrose remember her as 'a blonde lady'.
Although the painting was exhibited as recently as
1981, no photographic record exists.

102

MRS ROTHNIE
oil on canvas, c.1941-45
Provenance: in the collection of John Rothnie in 1950
Exhibited: Dundee 1950 (13)
The sitter was the wife of John Rothnie, a furrier by
trade and honorary secretary of the Montrose
Committee for the Encouragement of Music and the
Arts. He was heavily involved in the wartime
exhibitions in 1941-42. The portrait is likely to date
from this period. There is no photographic record of it
and its present whereabouts is unknown.

103

ANNA MARIA
Provenance: listed in the collection of Ann Baird in
1950, but the subsequent fate of the work is unknown
Exhibited: Dundee 1950 (31)
There is no information regarding the sitter, the
appearance of the work or whether it was a drawing or
a pastel.

104

MONTROSE FROM FERRYDEN
pencil on paper, c.1940-41
Provenance: listed in the collection of George
Fairweather, but it has since disappeared
Exhibited: Dundee 1950
This is a sketch for *63* above. Agnes Machir remembers
Baird working on this in his studio in 1941. Apparently
he wrote on the drawing the word 'Salorch', which is an
old name for Montrose.

NOTES

CHAPTER ONE

1   Conversation with Mrs Rona Pinterich, Glasgow, March 2002

2   A fuller account of the difficult relationship between Baird and Lamb can be found in Jake Stewart's unpublished Museum Studies MA thesis *William Lamb and Edward Baird*; see esp. p.38 (copies held at Montrose Museum and University of St. Andrews Art History library)

3   Conversations with Baird's relatives, March 2002

4   *Montrose Review* 30 March 1925

5   See McIntosh Patrick's *Memoir* above pp.83-4

6   Edward Baird, 'How Useful is Art?' ms. of lecture to Dundee Art Society, delivered between 1938 and 1940 (Montrose Museum Archives)

7   Ibid.

8   The National Party of Scotland was formally founded on 24 March 1928 in Glasgow with Grieve listed as a founder member (acc.3721, box 49, file 164, Scottish National Library, Edinburgh)

9   See Maurice Lindsay, *Francis George Scott and the Scottish Renaissance*, Paul Harris, Edinburgh, 1980, and Willa Muir, *Belonging: A Memoir*, London, 1968

CHAPTER TWO

1   Conversation with Mrs Jean Fraser, Largs, Spring 2003.

2   *Under the Dome* Montrose Academy school magazine, vol.4 (1915) & vol.5 (1916)

3   Baird and Miss Gaudie seem to have remained in touch after he left Montrose Academy; although no letters exist, correspondence dating from 1968 between Allan Ogilvie and Mrs Lena Cox, who had moved to Perth, discusses a memorial exhibition of Baird's work and some comments in the catalogue to which the correspondents seemed to object; the letters suggest that Lena Gaudie maintained a close interest in the life and work of her former pupil (Montrose Museum: Baird Archive)

4   Ann was born at 10 Union Place, Montrose; her father was a cabinet-maker and married her mother in Leith - it is not known when the Fairweathers moved to Montrose

5   cat. no.48

6   The Craig Hill School building still stands but has now been converted into a private dwelling; I am grateful to Graham Stephen for showing me the location of the former school and for a conversation regarding Walter Graham

7   Greiffenhagen was born in London in 1862 to Danish parents; he was a founder member of the New English Art Club and taught at Glasgow School of Art 1906-29, dying two years later in London at the age of 69

8   Glasgow School of Art Prospectus, session 1924-1925, p.7

9   Letter from Baird to Secretary, Glasgow School of Art 18 August 1926 (GSA archive); fellow student James A. Scott came from Perth and Baird had to travel by train to Perth before commencing the long journey south

10 See Francis Spalding *The Tate: A History*, London 1998; newly created galleries of French Realism, Impressionism and Post-Impressionism had opened at Millbank in the summer of 1926 amidst some controversy.

11 Conversations with Graham Stephen and Mary Conacher, March 2002.

12 McIntosh Patrick, op. cit., p.9

13 Glasgow School of Art Prospectus, session 1927-1928, p.19

14 Assessor's Reports 1926-1927 (GSA archive)

15 Letter to Secretary of Glasgow School of Art

25 November 1928 (GSA archive)

16 See Charles Harrison *English Art and Modernism 1900-39*, New Haven & London, 1981, chs 6 & 7, for a full account of the work of these painters in the 1920s; see also Jeremy Lewison & Virginia Button *Ben Nicholson*, London, 1993, pp.16-36, Jon Blackwood, *Winifred Nicholson*, Kettle's Yard, Cambridge, 2001, pp.18-33, and Richard Ingleby, *Christopher Wood*, London, 1998

17 Letter from Baird to Secretary of Glasgow School of Art 8 April 1929 (GSA archive)

18 Conversation with Mrs Jean Fraser, Largs, March 2002

19 The report was acknowledged as received by Glasgow School of Art on 21 October 1929; letter from Secretary to Baird (GSA archive)

CHAPTER THREE

1 *Montrose Review* 30 December 1927

2 For a full account of the Scottish Renaissance and its development in Scottish culture and politics in the inter-war years see Tom Normand *The Modern Scot: Modernism and Nationalism in Scottish Art 1928-55*, Aldershot, 2000, chs 1-3; see also Maurice Lindsay's *Francis George Scott and the Scottish Renaissance*, Edinburgh, 1980, pp.27-106.

3 Peter Lynch, *SNP: The History of the Scottish National Party*, Cardiff, 2002, pp.35-42

4 National Library of Scotland, acc.3721, box 49, file 164; National Party of Scotland records.

5 National Library of Scotland, acc.3721, box 88, file 15: National Party of Scotland records of Montrose Burghs by-election June-July 1932

6 Conversations with Mrs Rona Pinterich and Mrs Agnes Valentine, March & July 2002

7 This was confirmed by Mrs Rona Pinterich and Mrs Agnes Valentine in separate conversations

8 *Montrose Standard* 29 April 1932

9 Edwin Muir, *The Modern Scot*, vol.3 no.2, August 1932

10 'Montrose Artist's Royal Academy Picture - First Attempt Accepted - Mr. Baird Talks Art', *Angus and Mearns Herald*, n.d. (probably late April 1932)

11 James H. Whyte, 'The Royal Scottish Academy in 1933', *The Modern Scot*, vol.IV no.2, Summer 1933, pp.120-21.

12 For more information on the history of St. Kilda and its current status as a World Heritage Site managed by the National Trust for Scotland, see the official website at www.kilda.org.uk

13 *Montrose Review* 10 June 1932

14 Conversation with Patrick Elliott, March 2002

15 See McIntosh Patrick's *Memoir* above p.86

16 The most interesting analyses of Wadsworth's inter-war work can be found in Jeremy Lewison (ed.) *A Genius of Industrial England: Edward Wadsworth 1889-1949*, Arkwright Arts Trust & Bradford Art Galleries and Museums, Bradford, 1990, pp.66-107, and David Peters Corbett *The Modernity of English Art 1914-30*, Manchester, 1997, pp.179-87

17 'Montrose Art Exhibition: Pictures of Outstanding Merit on View', *Montrose Standard* 13 September 1935

18 *Montrose Review* 18 September 1935

19 Conversation with Mrs Agnes Valentine, 23 July 2002

20 The last issue of James H. Whyte's discussion journal of the Scottish Renaissance, *The Modern Scot*, appeared in January 1936 - it merged with the *Scottish Standard* to form the new cultural journal, *Outlook*, which limped on until disappearing the following year; Normand, op. cit., pp.50-62

CHAPTER FOUR

1 Letter from Allan Ogilvie to Mrs Lena Cox dated 7 June 1968 'I had some income tax work for Mrs Baird at different times and she was able to finance both her sons in good style'

2 I am grateful to Denis Rice and Francesca

Hardcastle for information relating to the chronology of MacColla's life

3 Jake Stewart, *William Lamb*, unpublished MA thesis, University of St. Andrews

4 Patrick Elliott, *Edward Baird 1904-49*, Scottish National Gallery of Modern Art, Edinburgh, 1992, p.11

5 Edward Baird, 'How Useful is Art?' ms. of lecture to Dundee Art Society, delivered between 1938 and 1940 (Montrose Museum Archives)

6 Ibid.

7 Ibid.

8 'The Art of Scotland', *The Studio*, vol.CXII, no.520, July 1936

9 Unidentified newspaper cutting, Montrose Museum archives - the 'critic' referred to may be John Tonge, who at the time was working on the *Dundee Courier*, while living in St. Andrews

10 See D. Morrison and I. Reynolds (eds.), *Changed Days in Montrose*, Montrose Old Kirk, Montrose, 1999, pp.46-63.

11 GM Thompson, *Scotland, That Distressed Area*, Porpoise Press, Edinburgh, 1935, pp.102-3

12 Patrick Elliott, op. cit., p.14

13 Letter from William Ogg to Graham Stephen, summer 2002 - Bill Ogg remembers meeting Baird at a children's party at the boating shed during the war; the author is very grateful to him for his recollections

14 Letter from Baird to George Fairweather, 1936 (Private Collection, Montrose)

15 Ibid.

16 'LDV Grimly Keeping Vigil all Night', *People's Journal & Angus Herald* 3 May 1941

17 Undated press cutting from the *Dundee Evening Telegraph*, reviewing the RSA exhibition of early summer 1939 (the brackets are the author's)

18 *The Spectator*, no. 5765, 23 December 1938

CHAPTER FIVE

1 An abridged version of this chapter was first presented as a conference paper at the Association of Art Historians' conference at Birkbeck College, London in June 2003; the text of that paper, 'Local Defence Volunteer: The Painting and Criticism of Edward Baird 1939-45' is available on-line at www.waspjournals.com/AOTL

2 See D. Morrison & I. Reynolds, *Changed Days in Montrose* II, Montrose Old Kirk, Montrose, 1999

3 During 1939-40 Montrose was a training base for the RAF; during the Battle of Britain it was a rest and re-fit base for fighter squadrons that had suffered severe casualties

4 A German Heinkel 111 was downed by fighters of No. 603 (City of Edinburgh) Squadron whilst on a reconnaissance mission over the River Forth on 16 October 1939

5 Nicholson served in the Home Guard in St. Ives throughout the war.

6 Kenneth Clark, 'Art for the People', *The Listener*, 23 November 1939, pp.99-101.

7 'LDV Grimly Keeping Vigil All Night', *Dundee Evening Telegraph*, 3 May 1941

8 '*LDV* in the Royal Academy - Local Artist's Striking Portrait', *Montrose Review* 2 May 1941

9 'Air Raids on Montrose', *Montrose Standard* 16 January 1942 - this devastating raid is still a vivid memory for Montrosians who remember the war years; Mrs Elizabeth Walker recalls as a small child being pulled into a shop doorway by a policeman to avoid the German aircraft's bullets (conversation with the author July 2002)

10 Ibid.

11 Information kindly related by Mrs Rona Pinterich - Peter Machir's daughters regularly visited Baird at 121c High Street in wartime and recall the painting of this work, largely because of the rare sight of a bowl of fresh fruit then; the artist

wanted the children to have a piece of fruit at each visit, but was over-ruled by his mother, who it appears could not bear the thought of scarce food 'going to waste', but in the end Baird's painting took so long to finish that the fruit rotted uneaten (conversation with the author March 2002)

12 'Montrosian's Success in the World of Art', *Montrose Standard*, 3 May 1940

13 The author is grateful to Mrs Agnes Valentine for this information - she was a frequent visitor to Baird's home and studio during the war and it is she who alerted me to the existence of the Salorch drawing (conversation with the author July 2002)

14 *Montrose Review* 2 May 1941

15 'Large Gathering at Modern Art Exhibtion', *Montrose Standard* 11 July 1941

16 'Local Artist's Outspoken Criticism', *Montrose Standard* 11 July 1941

17 Ibid.

18 'Over 1,500 Adults Visited Art Exhibition - Complete Success of Wartime Venture -Talk by Mr. Baird', *Montrose Standard* 2 August 1941

19 These children have been identified as Andrew Coull's son, Jim, and daughter, Cathy, and brothers Ronald and David West (Montrose Museum Archive, Baird file)

20 *Montrose Standard* 2 August 1941

21 'Town Council should purchase Works of Art', *Montrose Review* 22 August 1941

22 *The Listener*, vol.25, no.643, 8 May 1941

23 Conversation with Mrs Rona Pinterich, March 2002

24 John Tonge, 'Scottish Paintings', *Horizon* vol.V, no.29, May 1942, p.331

25 'Art Exhibition: More than Thousand Visitors during the week', *Montrose Standard* 2 September 1942

26 Draft of unsent letter from Baird to John Tonge dated 20 December 1942

27 Imperial War Museum War Artists' File GP/55/276. Letter from Baird to WAAC, 1 December 1942

28 Draft of unsent letter from Baird to Dan Crosse dated 17 February 1941 (private collection)

29 Baird submitted *K. Bennett* on 16 August 1943 - he was originally due to sketch a Miss Catherine Munro, who worked in a munitions factory at Powfoot in Dumfriesshire, but this was cancelled when Miss Munro departed on special leave; the unidentified *Clydeside Munitions Worker* was assigned as a replacement and this was submitted on 27 November 1943; his final work, *Barbara Garth BEM*, was finished on 14 April 1944; Mrs Garth, a charge hand at the Royal Ordinance Factory, received her medal on 1 June 1944 and was gazetted the same day (IWM War Artists File)

30 T.J. Honeyman, 'Art in Scotland', *The Studio*, vol.CXXVI, no.606, p. 65

CHAPTER SIX

1 T. Elder Dickson, 'The East Coast Painters' in *Scottish Art and Letters*, no.2, Spring 1946, p.31

2 See F. Spencer Chapman, *Northern Lights: The Official Account of the British Arctic Air Route Exhibition*, London, 1932, chapter entitled 'The Art of Kayaking', esp. pp.205-10

3 *Montrose Review* 7 January 1949

4 Peter Machir died in 1954; the letter from Ann to Mrs Machir is in a private collection

5 Lamb had served with the Queen's Own Highlanders during World War I. His right hand was badly damaged by shrapnel and he was invalided back to London. There a surgeon badly bungled an operation to repair the damage and as a result Lamb was left permanently disabled in his right hand. This engendered a lifelong suspicion and mistrust of doctors and Lamb refused to go to hospital after the accident at the Victoria Galleries. By the time he did see a doctor the damage to his spleen and liver was found to be fatal and he died in March 1951 (for a chronological sketch of Lamb's life see www.angus.gov.uk/history/features/people/lamb1.htm)

6 *Montrose Standard and Angus and Mearns Register* 13 June 1950

7 John Tonge, *Daily Record* 12 June 1950

8 The only confirmed sale that the author has been able to verify was the 1940 still-life *Flower Piece*, which is now in a private collection in England

PHOTO CREDITS

The Fleming-Wyfold Art Foundation and the author are grateful to the following bodies for permission to reproduce images of works of art in their care:

Aberdeen Art Gallery & Museums
  catalogue numbers 55, 56, 65

Angus Council Cultural Services
  catalogue numbers 35, 60, 63
  photograph on page 30

Dundee City Council Leisure & Arts: McManus Galleries
  catalogue number 50

Glasgow Museums: Art Gallery & Museum, Kelvingrove
  catalogue number 68

Paisley Museum & Art Gallery, Renfrewshire
  catalogue number 76

Scottish National Gallery of Modern Art, Edinburgh
  catalogue numbers 47, 59, 74
  photographs on pages 2 & 44

Scottish National Portrait Gallery, Edinburgh
  catalogue number 48

Tate Britain, London
  photographs on pages 43 & 51

Grateful thanks are also due to Archivio Scala, Florence for an illustration on page 43 and to all those private collectors who wish to remain anonymous for permission to reproduce their works of art.

BIBLIOGRAPHY

Unpublished Sources

Edward Baird, *How Useful is Art*, unpublished lecture to Dundee Art Society, c.1938-40 (ms. held at Montrose Museum, Angus District Museum Services)

Edward Baird letters, documents & personal effects (Montrose Museum)

Edward Baird file, Angus Local Studies Centre, Montrose Public Library

Edward Baird letters, documents, personal effects and memorabilia (family collections)

Edward Baird's records, Glasgow School of Art, c.1924-1929

Edward Baird file, Scottish National Gallery of Modern Art, Edinburgh

Edward Baird file, Scottish Arts Council, Edinburgh

Edward Baird war artist's records 1942-44 (Imperial War Museum, London: War Artists' Archive, File GP/55/276)

Fionn MacColla letters (National Library of Scotland, Edinburgh & private collections)

Hugh MacDiarmid letters (University of Edinburgh Library & National Library of Scotland, Edinburgh)

James H. Whyte letters (National Library of Scotland, Edinburgh)

National Party of Scotland/Scottish National Party Archives (National Library of Scotland, Edinburgh)

Jon Blackwood, *'Local Defence Volunteer': the Painting and Criticism of Edward Baird, 1939-45*, unpublished paper delivered at the Association of Art Historians Annual Conference, Birkbeck College, University of London, April 2003

Jake Stewart, *William Lamb*, unpublished MA thesis, University of St. Andrews

Published Sources

Edward Baird 1904-1949, Scottish Arts Council, Edinburgh, 1950

Edward Baird and William Lamb, Scottish Arts Council, Edinburgh, 1968

Edward Baird, Montrose Public Library, Montrose, 1981

James McIntosh Patrick, Aberdeen Art Gallery, Aberdeen, 1985

Alan Bold, *MacDiarmid*, London, 1990

Alan Bold, *The Letters of Hugh MacDiarmid*, London, 1984

John Byrne, *Colquhoun and MacBryde*, London, 1993

G. Bryan, *Scottish Nationalism and Cultural Identity in the Twentieth Century: An Annotated Bibliography of Secondary Sources*, London, 1984

F. Spencer Chapman, *Northern Lights: The Official Account of the British Arctic Air Route Exhibition*, London, 1932

Stanley Cursiter, *Scottish Art*, London, 1949

T. Elder Dickson, 'The East Coast Painters', *Scottish Art and Letters*, no.2, 1945

Patrick Elliott, *Edward Baird 1904-49*, Scottish Masters Series, National Galleries of Scotland, Edinburgh, 1992

R. Erskine, *Changing Scotland*, Montrose, 1931

Duncan Glen, *Hugh MacDiarmid and the Scottish Renaissance*, Edinburgh, 1964

Duncan Glen (ed.), *Selected Essays of Hugh MacDiarmid*, London, 1968

Lewis Grassic Gibbon & Hugh MacDiarmid, *Scottish Scene: or the Intelligent Man's Guide to Albyn*, London, 1934

William Hardie, *Scottish Painting 1837 to the present*, London, 1990

Paul Harris and Julian Halsby, *The Dictionary of Scottish Painters 1600 to the Present*, Edinburgh, 1998

Keith Hartley, *Scottish Art since 1900*, National Galleries of Scotland, Edinburgh, 1989

H. Harvey Wood, 'Contemporary Painting and Sculpture', *The Studio*, vol.cxii no.520, August 1930

T.J. Honeyman, 'Art in Scotland', *The Studio*, Scottish Number, CXXVI, 1943

G. Harvie & P. Jones, *The Road to Home Rule: Images of Scotland's Cause*, Edinburgh, 1999

C.B. de Laperriere, *The Royal Scottish Academy Exhibitors 1826-1990*, Calne, 1991

Maurice Lindsay, *Francis George Scott and the Scottish Renaissance*, Edinburgh, 1980

Michael Lynch, *Scotland: A History*, London, 1994

Fionn MacColla, *The Albannach*, London, 1932

Fionn MacColla, *And the Cock Crew*, Glasgow, 1945

Fionn MacColla, *Too Long in this Condition*, Thurso, 1975

Hugh MacDiarmid, *Selected Poems*, London, 1994

Hugh MacDiarmid, *Albyn or Scotland and the Future*, London, 1927

Hugh MacDiarmid, *Lucky Poet*, Edinburgh, 1978

Hugh MacDiarmid, *Aesthetics in Scotland*, Edinburgh, 1984

Murdo MacDonald, *Scottish Art*, London, 2000

Duncan Macmillan, *Scottish Art 1460-2000*, Edinburgh, 2000

Duncan Macmillan, *Scottish Art in the Twentieth Century*, Edinburgh, 1994

David Morrison (ed.), *Essays on Fionn MacColla*, Thurso, 1973

D. Morrison & I. Reynolds (eds.), *Changed Days in Montrose*, Montrose Old Kirk, Montrose, 1999

Willa Muir, *Belonging: A Memoir*, London, 1968

Tom Normand, *The Modern Scot: Modernism and Nationalism in Scottish Art*, Aldershot, 2000

P. Scott & A.D. Davies (eds.), *The Age of MacDiarmid*, Edinburgh, 1980

George Malcolm Thompson, *Scotland, that Distressed Area*, Edinburgh, 1935

John Tonge, *The Arts of Scotland*, London, 1938

John Tonge, 'Scottish Painting', *Horizon*, May 1942

John Tonge, 'Dundee is the first to honour Edward Baird', *Daily Record*, 12 June 1950

James H. Whyte, *Towards a New Scotland*, London, 1935

NEWSPAPERS, JOURNALS, YEARBOOKS

Angus and Mearns Herald
Apollo
Artwork
The Burlington Magazine
The Daily Record
Dundee Courier
Dundee Evening Telegraph
The Glasgow Herald
Horizon
The Listener
The Modern Scot
The Montrose Review
The Montrose Standard
The Montrose Yearbook
Northern Numbers
Outlook
Royal Academy Yearbook
The Scots Independent
The Scotsman
The Scottish Chapbook
The Scottish Standard
The Studio

ON-LINE RESOURCES

www.angus.gov.uk/artists/baird.html - Angus Council Cultural Services web page
www.scran.ac.uk - Scottish Cultural Resources Access Network